SUCCESS

Communicating
in
English

Michael Walker

Bonus Practice Book

1

Addison-Wesley Publishing Company
Reading, Massachusetts · Menlo Park, California · New York
Don Mills, Ontario · Wokingham, England · Amsterdam · Bonn
Sydney · Singapore · Tokyo · Madrid · San Juan · Paris
Seoul, Korea · Milan · Mexico City · Taipei, Taiwan

Dear Teacher,

Welcome to *Success* and the *Bonus Practice Book*. Traditionally, workbooks have been used as reinforcement for material presented in the textbook. Unfortunately, there has usually not been enough material to satisfy the needs of ambitious students. With a page-for-page correlation to the Textbook, this Bonus Practice Book offers plenty of reinforcement and in addition, your students will find lots of enrichment, challenge, and fun in these 128 pages.

Reading

Keep in mind that your students are adults. They are used to dealing with print. They are anxious to learn as much and as quickly as possible in this course. If you look closely at the sentences on the opening spreads, what you will really find is lots of repetition. This extra practice allows students to solidify what they've learned in the Textbook lesson and to feel that they've really "got it."

New Vocabulary

New vocabulary is the easiest thing for students to handle. By giving them an abundance of vocabulary to use with the limited number of structures they've learned, students feel motivated and excited. They feel they can say a lot and will be more likely to participate in class, or try their English out in a real situation.

Crossword Puzzles

Crossword puzzles are great conversation starters. As a class activity, crosswords stimulate discussion. Students can read the clues aloud, offer guesses as to the answer, count spaces to check their ideas, and so on. You can also have students work in pairs, using their Textbooks to help them. Not only will they be talking, they'll be thinking, as various clues *eliminate* or *illuminate* the answers. (The Bay City News crossword puzzles at the end of each unit may be more challenging, but usually the clues are taken directly from the Textbook. Students should feel free to postpone working on them until later in the course if they want to.)

The Best Ways to Use the Bonus Practice Book

- Work the pages in class, treating the Bonus Practice Book as basically an extension of the Textbook.
- Introduce the pages in class, and then assign them as pairwork or individual homework.
- Assign certain activities, crosswords for example, as in-class pairwork, which gives you a nice opportunity to monitor students' spoken and written work.
- Have students work on their own, especially in the Review section of each unit, as a form of self-evaluation.

Here's wishing you and your students . . . what else? *Success!*

Michael Walker

A Publication of the ESL Publishing Group

Contributing Writer/Product Development Director: Judith M. Bittinger
Executive Editor/Project Director: Elinor Chamas
Editorial Development: Karen Doyle
Design/Typesetting: Beckwith-Clark, Inc.
Cover Design: Marshall Henrichs
Production/Manufacturing: James W. Gibbons
Illustrators: Meg Kelleher Aubrey, Kathy Kelleher, Dave Sullivan

ISBN 0-201-59515-X
3 4 5 6 7 8 9 10 - CRS - 98 97 96 95 94 93

CONTENTS

A. Look at the map. Discuss the map.

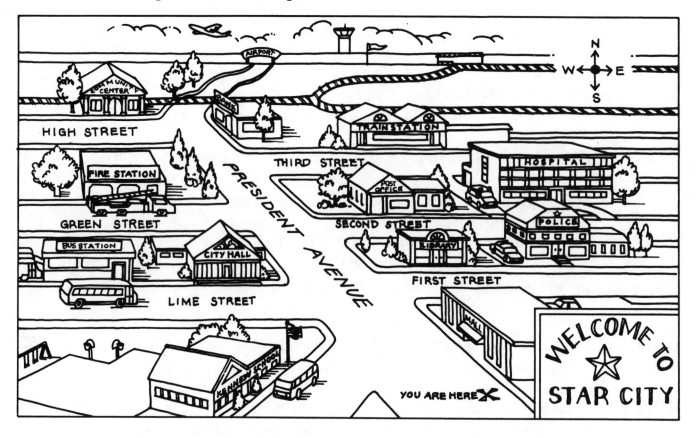

B. Read the crossword clues.

DOWN

1. Kennedy School is in Star _____ .
3. The _____ is on Second Street.
5. The train station is on _____ Street.
6. Where's the post office, _____ ?
7. Lime Street is the first street on the _____ .
10. _____ you.
    You're welcome.
13. The Community _____ is on High Street.
16. Thank you.
    You're _____ .
18. The post _____ is on Second Street.
22. The _____ Center is on High Street.
25. The _____ is on First Street.
26. High Street is the _____ street on the left.

ACROSS

2. Third Street is the third street on the _____ .
4. The _____ is north of the city.
8. The City _____ is on Lime Street.
9. It's the second _____ on the right.
11. Excuse me, _____ is the hospital?
12. It's the _____ street on the right.
14. First, _____ , third.
15. Excuse _____ .
17. The police _____ is on First Street.
19. Where's _____ hospital?
20. The _____ station is on Green Street.
21. _____ me.
23. The _____ station is on First Street.
24. The _____ is on President Avenue.
27. The train _____ is on Third Street.

C. Use the map and the clues. Fill in the crossword puzzle.

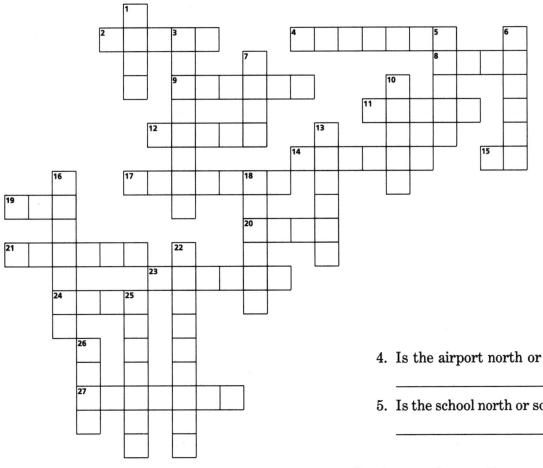

4. Is the airport north or south of Star City?

_____

5. Is the school north or south of the bank?

_____

D. True ⊤ or False Ⓕ ?

1. High Street is the first street on the left.   [F] [ ]

2. Third Street is the third street on the right.   [ ] [ ]

3. First Street is the first street on the right.   [ ] [ ]

4. Second Street is the second street on the left.   [ ] [ ]

5. Green Street is the second street on the right.   [ ] [ ]

E. Alternatives

1. Is the mall on First Street or President Avenue?
   The mall is on President Avenue.

2. Is the post office on Third St. or Second St.?

   _____

3. Is the fire station on Green St. or Lime St.?

   _____

F. Answer the questions.

1. Where is the train station?
   The train station is on Third Street.

2. Where is the community center?

   _____

3. Where is the hospital?

   _____

4. Where is the City Hall?

   _____

5. Where is the bank?

   _____

G. Complete the conversation.

Excuse me. Where is the library?

_____

First Street? Where's First Street?

_____

The first street on the right. Thank you.

_____

VOCABULARY BUILDING

A. Addition (plus)

4 + 7 = 11   Four plus seven is eleven.

1. 1 + 3 = 4 _____
2. 2 + 1 = 3 _____
3. 3 + 8 = 11 _____
4. 4 + 4 = 8 _____
5. 5 + 4 = 9 _____

B. Subtraction (minus)

12 − 9 = 3   Twelve minus nine is three.

1. 9 − 2 = 7 _____
2. 8 − 3 = 5 _____
3. 11 − 2 = 9 _____
4. 6 − 6 = 0 _____
5. 12 − 5 = 7 _____

C. Multiplication (times)

2 × 1 = 2   Two times one is two.

1. 4 × 2 = 8 _____
2. 3 × 3 = 9 _____
3. 4 × 3 = 12 _____
4. 3 × 2 = 6 _____
5. 5 × 2 = 10 _____

D. Division (divided by)

12 ÷ 2 = 6   Twelve divided by two is six.

1. 12 ÷ 3 = 4 _____
2. 9 ÷ 3 = 3 _____
3. 10 ÷ 2 = 5 _____
4. 6 ÷ 3 = 2 _____
5. 8 ÷ 2 = 4 _____

E. **Fill in the crossword. All of the answers are number words. There are no clues. The four T's can help you!**

A. Read the sentences. Follow the example.

My name is **Mary Smith.**
My room is on the **third floor.**
I can say, **"Room three one three,"** or
I can say, **"Room three thirteen."**

Three one three   or   Three thirteen

1. Three one one   _____
2. Five one six   _____
3. Four one eight   _____
4. Six one three   _____
5. Seven one nine   _____
6. One one two   _____
7. Seven one seven   _____
8. Nine one four   _____
9. One one five   _____

B. Make conversations.

Jane Fox, please.
     Room **thirteen thirteen.**
1313?
     Yes, **1313** on the **thirteenth floor.**
Thank you.
     You're welcome.

20th	twentieth	Tom Jones	2013
19th	nineteenth	Judy Brown	1901
18th	eighteenth	Karen Doyle	1809
17th	seventeenth	Andrea Patch	1711
16th	sixteenth	Ellie Conley	1615
15th	fifteenth	Bob Kirby	1512
14th	fourteenth	James West	1406
13th	thirteenth	Jane Fox	1313
12th	twelfth	Eve Nelson	1219
11th	eleventh	Jeff West	1103
10th	tenth	Kim Lee	1010
9th	ninth	Ann Perry	918
8th	eighth	Dick Elliot	804
7th	seventh	Lisa Roth	715
6th	sixth	Juan Arnez	609
5th	fifth	Joanne Beckett	515
4th	fourth	Sean Chung	413
3rd	third	Mary Smith	313
2nd	second	Jill Jackson	217
1st	first	Bill Porter	111
Ground floor		Reception	

CONVERSATION

A. Complete the conversation.

Good morning.

_____

This is Ms. Brown.

_____

I'm pleased to meet you.

_____

Fine, thanks. And you?

_____

I'm glad to hear that.

B. Choose the correct alternatives.

1. Good morning, Miss Pink.
   a) Great!
   b) Goodbye!
   c) Good morning.

2. Nice to meet you.
   a) Fine thanks.
   b) Hi!
   c) Pleased to meet you.

3. Let me introduce Mr. Black.
   a) Excuse me.
   b) Pleased to meet you.
   c) Just fine, thanks.

4. See you later!
   a) Good morning.
   b) Good evening.
   c) Take care.

5. How are you?
   a) Great!
   b) My name's Mary.
   c) So long!

6. How's it going?
   a) Glad to hear that.
   b) Not so good.
   c) And you?

C. Make a conversation.

You meet your friend Mary in the afternoon.
She is fine. You are fine too.
Mary is with a new friend, Susan Gale.
Susan is fine too.

You: _____

Mary: _____

You: _____

Mary: _____

You: _____

Mary: _____

You: _____

Susan: _____

You: _____

Susan: _____

You: _____

VOCABULARY BUILDING

A. Make new conversations.

How's it going?
   Not so good.
What's the problem?
   My **back** hurts.
I'm sorry to hear that.

1. back

2. arm

3. foot

4. nose

5. neck

6. thumb

B. Make new conversations.

How's it going?
   Not so good.
What's the problem?
   I have **a cold.**
I'm sorry to hear that.

1. a cold

2. a headache

3. a sore throat

4. a toothache

5. a backache

6. an earache

A. Answer the questions.

1. What time is it?

   It's quarter past three.

2. What time is it?

   _____

3. What time is it?

   _____

4. What time is it?

   _____

5. What time is it?

   _____

6. What time is it?

   _____

D. True ☐T☐ or False ☐F☐ ?

ARRIVALS	Gate	Due	Actual
Miami	74	1:00	1:30
Chicago	56	11:15	11:00
Boston	33	11:55	12:05
Houston	19	4:30	4:15

DEPARTURES	Gate	Due	Actual
New York	46	12:20	12:55
Dallas	78	1:23	1:23
Seattle	99	2:50	2:59
Atlanta	28	7:30	7:50

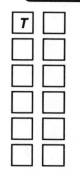

1. The flight from Houston is early.   ☐T☐ ☐
2. The next plane to Atlanta is at 7:30.   ☐ ☐
3. The Boston flight is late.   ☐ ☐
4. The flight to Seattle is at 2:50.   ☐ ☐
5. The Miami flight is due at 1:00.   ☐ ☐
6. The flight from Dallas is on time.   ☐ ☐

VOCABULARY BUILDING

A. Make new conversations.

What time is it?
  It's four o'clock.
Are you sure?
  Yes, I'm sure.
The clock in the **church** is **five** minutes **fast**.
  And the clock in the **town hall** is **five**
  minutes **slow**.

town hall

church

1. fire station

bus station

2. library

train station

3. community center

airport

4. police station

mall

5. school

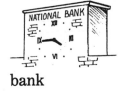
bank

6. hospital

Community College

B. Fill in the names of the numbers.
The T's will help you.

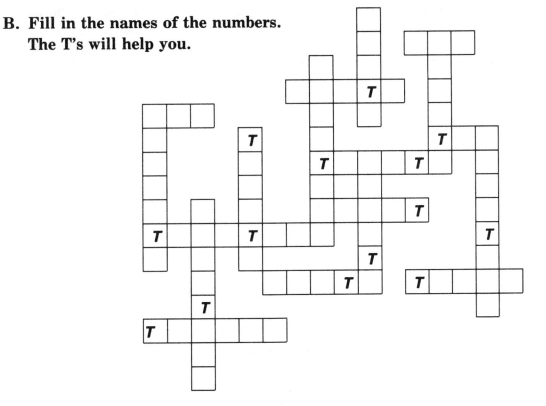

READING COMPREHENSION

A. Read the note from Jane.

> Hi!
> Please come to my new home!
> If you come by car from New York, take the first street on the left, Miller Street. Then take the second street on the right, Baker Street. At the end of Baker Street, turn left onto Mechanic Avenue. My house is on the left, next to the church.
>
> Love,
> Jane

B. Look at the map. Follow the directions to Jane's new home.

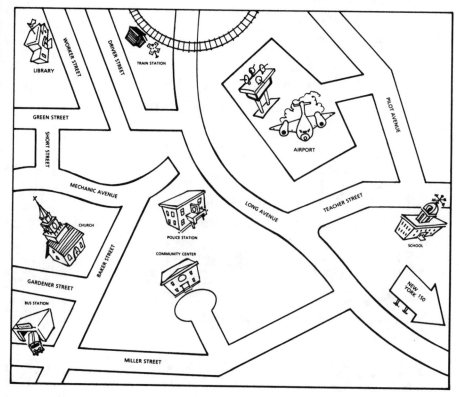

C. Answer the questions.

1. Give directions from the bus station to Jane's house.
   Take a left on Baker Street. At the end of Baker Street, turn left on Mechanic Avenue.

2. Give directions from the train station to Jane's house.

3. Give directions from the airport to Jane's house.

4. Give directions from the community center to Jane's house.

5. Give directions from the library to Jane's house.

6. Give directions from the police station to Jane's house.

REVIEW
VOCABULARY

A. Write the words for the numbers.

11. _eleven_   14. _____   40. _____

12. _____   15. _____   30. _____

13. _____   16. _____   50. _____

1st. _____   4th. _____   10th. _____

2nd. _____   5th. _____   14th. _____

3rd. _____   6th. _____   20th. _____

CONVERSATION

B. Choose the best alternatives.

1. Good morning, Ms. Brown.
   a) Hi.
   b) Good morning.
   c) I'm glad to hear that.
2. Bye, now!
   a) Great, and you?
   b) See you later.
   c) Hello.

3. So long!
   a) Take care!
   b) I'm sorry to hear that.
   c) Not so good.
4. Pleased to meet you.
   a) Fine, thanks.
   b) Happy to meet you.
   c) Good morning.

5. This is Mary.
   a) Hi, Mary.
   b) So long, Mary.
   c) Bye, Mary.
6. How's it going?
   a) This is Mr. Gray.
   b) Good, thanks.
   c) That's good.

WHAT TIME IS IT?

C. Write the time in two different ways.

1. 3:45   _It is three forty five._
            It is quarter to four.

2. 5:10   _____

3. 3:25   _____

4. 9:15   _____

5. 8:40   _____

6. 12:55   _____

VOCABULARY BUILDING

A. Complete the sentences. There are new words here so try your best!

1. The doctor is in the _____ .
   a) town hall
   b) hospital
   c) shoe store

2. You can borrow a book at the _____ .
   a) library
   b) book store
   c) city hall

3. You can buy shoes at the _____ .
   a) museum
   b) mall
   c) station

4. You can rent a room at the _____ .
   a) fire station
   b) police station
   c) hotel

5. You can buy bread at the _____ .
   a) bus station
   b) bakery
   c) hospital

CONVERSATION

B. Make a conversation.

You are at the airport.
It is seven o'clock in the morning.
The next plane to Dallas is at half past seven.
It is not on time.
It is twenty minutes late.
It is at Gate 28.

When _____

_____

What time _____ now?

_____

Is the _____
   No, _____

How late _____

_____

Which _____

_____

Thank _____
   You're _____

BAY CITY NEWS CROSSWORD

Fill in the crossword puzzle. Use textbook pages 13–15 for help.

DOWN

1. Not female.
2. Good _____ at Phil's Diner.
5. _____ house, two bedrooms.
6. Bart Whitehead, 15 years as Police _____ .
8. All you can _____ for $6.95.
9. There are 104 candles on Anna's _____ .
10. Marcia is a school _____ .
11. There are 104 _____ on Anna's cake.
12. Not male.
13. The mall is big and _____ .
14. Dot Green says the mall is _____ .
17. Low _____ .
20. Clerk: Walker Shoes _____ 6–9
22. Female 22 seeking _____ male.

ACROSS

3. _____ male seeking pretty female.
4. Small _____ for rent.
7. Dinner specials, come _____ 5:30.
9. My English class is at the _____ .
15. Dot Green says the mall is _____ .
16. Anthony Michael Horne, _____ June 4th.
18. Tony and Jill are Anthony's _____ .
19. _____ Dinner Specials before 5:30.
21. Dot Green says the mall is too _____ .
23. English is the _____ of international business.
24. English has about 1,000,000 _____ .
25. Attractive male seeking _____ female.

15

A. Look at the map of the mall. Discuss the map.

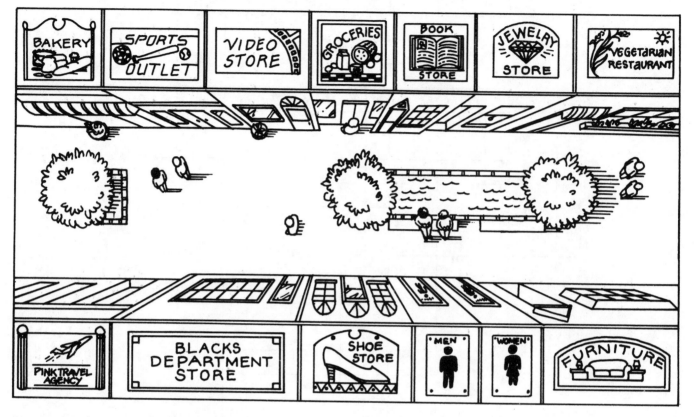

B. Read the crossword clues.

DOWN

1. See the _____ and yellow sign? That's the grocery store.
3. The grocery store is _____ to the bookstore.
5. See the purple sign? _____ is the jewelry store.
6. The _____ store is next to the bookstore.
7. The _____ store is next to the grocery store.
9. The sports _____ is next to the video store.
11. The _____ agency is next to the department store.
13. See you in five _____ !
15. The grocery store has a _____ and orange sign.
16. The video _____ is next to the sports outlet.
18. The travel agency has a _____ sign.
20. The _____ store is next to the department store.
21. The department store has a _____ sign.
23. See the _____ sign next to the restrooms? That is the furniture store.
24. See the _____ sign? That's the bookstore.

ACROSS

2. The bookstore is next to the orange and yellow _____ .
4. The jewelry store has a _____ sign.
5. The grocery store is next _____ the bookstore.
8. See the _____ sign? That is the vegetarian restaurant.
10. The vegetarian _____ is next to the jewelry store.
12. Meet me _____ ten minutes.
13. _____ me at the vegetarian restaurant.
14. See that pink sign? That is the travel _____ .
17. The _____ store is next to the travel agency.
19. See the _____ door? That is the restroom for men.
20. The _____ outlet is next to the video store.
21. See the _____ shoe sign? That's the shoe store.
22. See the _____ door? That is the restroom for women.
23. The _____ is next to the sports outlet.
25. The _____ store is next to the grocery store.
26. The _____ store is next to the restroom for women.

C. Use the map and the clues. Fill in the crossword puzzle.

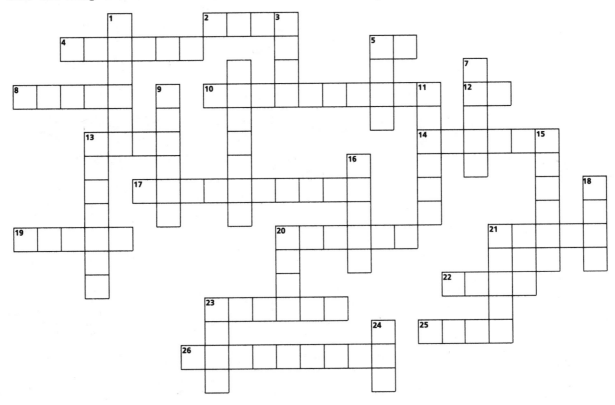

D. True $\boxed{T}$ or False $\boxed{F}$?

1. The video store is next to the bakery. $\quad\square\;\boxed{F}$
2. The jewelry store is next to the bookstore. $\quad\square\;\square$
3. The restroom for men is next to the department store. $\quad\square\;\square$
4. The bookstore is next to the vegetarian restaurant. $\quad\square\;\square$
5. The restroom for women is next to the furniture store. $\quad\square\;\square$

E. Alternatives

1. Is the video store next to the sports outlet or the bakery?
   It is next to the sports outlet.
   _____

2. Is the shoe store next to the restrooms or the travel agency?
   _____

3. Is the vegetarian restaurant next to the bookstore or the jewelry store?
   _____

4. Is the department store next to the travel agency or the shoe store?
   _____

5. Is the shoe store next to the grocery store or the restrooms?
   _____

A. Fill in with *He, She,* or *It*.

1. Where is Mr. Chung? _____He_____ is at the video store.

2. Where is Mrs. Tizz? _____ is at the shoe store.

3. Where is the bus? _____ is at the bus stop.

4. Where is the cat? _____ is in the tree.

B. Make questions and answers.

Peter/bus stop   *Where is Peter?*
    He is at the bus stop.

1. Mary/yard

2. your sister/school

3. your cat/car

4. your wife/gas station

A. Make questions and answers.

your sister/22
How old is your sister?
She is twenty-two years old.

1. your brother/15

   _____

   _____

2. your car/8

   _____

   _____

3. your father/54

   _____

   _____

4. your mother/49

   _____

   _____

5. your town/250

   _____

   _____

6. you/24

   _____

   _____

7. Peter and Mary/36

   _____

   _____

8. you and your sister/43

   _____

   _____

B. Fill in with _He, She, It, We, They,_ or _I._

1. How old are you? _____I_____ am five years old.
2. How old is Tom? _____ is eight years old.
3. How old is Mary? _____ is eleven years old.
4. How old are Jack and Jill? _____ are fifty years old.
5. How old are you two? _____ are twenty years old.
6. How old is your house? _____ is sixty years old.

CONVERSATION

A. Complete the conversation.

How much is this jacket?

_____

Really? How much is it?

_____

That's a big reduction. But how much is it?

_____

Yes, I know it's cheap. But how much is it?

_____

That's expensive! But I'll take it.

_____

Cash.

B. Choose the correct alternatives.

1. May I help you?
   a) Yes, it is.
   b) Really?
   c) Yes, please.
2. This dress is on sale.
   a) May I help you?
   b) Really?
   c) Yes, it is.

3. How much is this tie?
   a) It's on sale.
   b) It's a big reduction.
   c) Nine ninety-nine.
4. This hat is eighty-nine dollars
   a) It's cheap, but I'll take it.
   b) It's a big reduction, but I'll take it.
   c) It's expensive, but I'll take it.

C. Make a conversation.

You are in a store.   It is 20% off.
You want a jacket.   It is forty dollars.
It is on sale.   You pay cash.

Clerk: _____

You: _____

Clerk: _____

You: _____

Clerk: _____

You: _____

Clerk: _____

You: _____

Clerk: _____

You: _____

VOCABULARY BUILDING

Make conversations.

How much is **this shirt?**
  It is $9.00.
Fine, I'll take it.

How much are **these shoes?**
  They are $18.00.
Fine, I'll take them.

VOCABULARY BUILDING

A. Complete the family tree.

son
son-in-law
father
father-in-law
grandfather
husband
brother
uncle
nephew

daughter
daughter-in-law
mother
mother-in-law
grandmother
wife
sister
aunt
niece

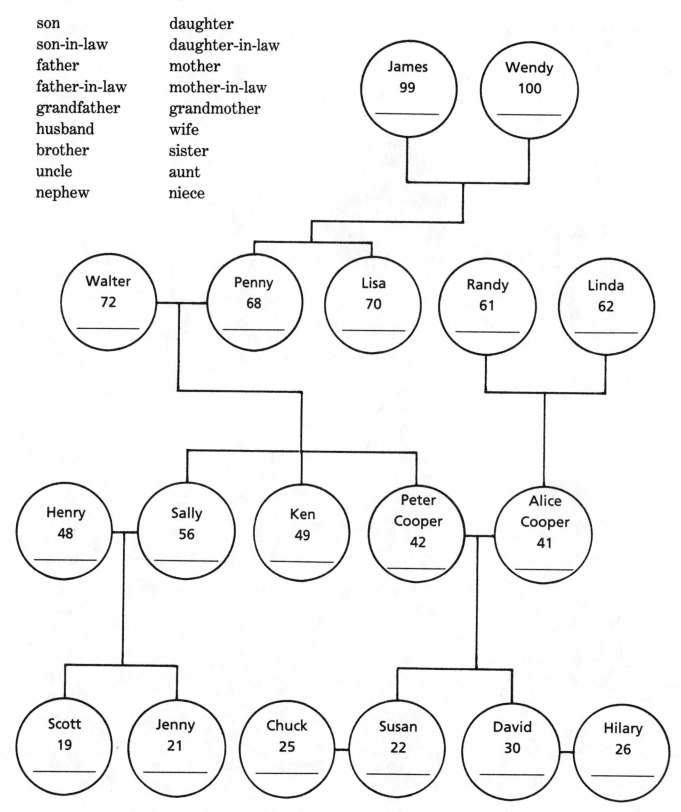

B. Answer the questions.

How old is Peter? _He is forty-two._

1. How old is his wife? _____

2. How old is his father? _____

3. How old is his mother? _____

Is his son twenty or thirty? _He is thirty._

4. Is his daughter twenty-two or twenty-three? _____

5. Is his brother forty-seven or forty-nine? _____

6. Is his grandmother ninety or a hundred? _____

Is his nephew ten? _No, he's not. He is nineteen._

7. Is his niece thirteen? _____

8. Is his son-in-law twenty-nine? _____

9. Is his mother-in-law sixty? _____

C. Read this.

My name is Alice Cooper. I am forty-one years old.
My husband is forty-two. His name is Peter.
My daughter is twenty-two. Her name is Susan.

D. Add as much information as you can.

My name is Peter Cooper.

_____

_____

_____

_____

My name is James Blake.

_____

_____

_____

_____

READING COMPREHENSION

I am twenty-one years old.
You are twenty-one years old, too.
We are both twenty-one years old.

Tim is five years old.
His sister is five years old, too.
The house is five years old, too.
They are all five years old.

A. Fill in with *is, am,* or *are.*

James _____ *is* _____ not at home. He _____ in town. He _____ in the

shopping mall. His sister _____ there, too. They _____ both in the video

store.

James and I _____ very good friends. We _____ both eighteen. We

_____ very interested in movies.

Susan _____ not interested in the same videos as James and I. She _____

interested in videos for children. She _____ only four years old.

When I _____ with James, we _____ both very happy. But Susan

_____ not happy when I _____ with James. I _____ Susan's rival!

She _____ jealous.

B. Write about your own family.

Write about your parents, your children, your relatives.
Write about your house.

What are you interested in?
What is your best friend interested in?
What are you both interested in?

REVIEW
VOCABULARY

A. Write the words for the pictures.

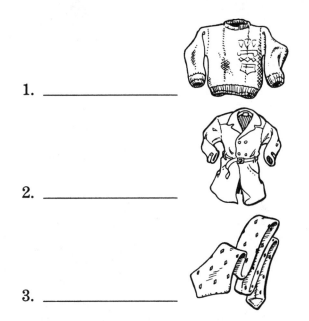

1. _____

2. _____

3. _____

4. _____

5. _____

6. _____

B. Choose the correct alternatives.

1. It's on sale.
   a) I'm sorry to hear that.
   b) Really? How much is it?
   c) Cash or charge?

2. It's $2,999.
   a) That's expensive.
   b) That's cheap.
   c) So what's the price?

3. Cash or charge?
   a) I'll take it.
   b) It's thirty percent off.
   c) Charge, of course.

4. How much are these socks?
   a) It is 30% off.
   b) They are very cheap.
   c) It is very expensive.

5. This blouse is only $5.
   a) Fine, I'll take them.
   b) Fine, I'll take it.
   c) Fine, these are great!

6. Is this tie on sale?
   a) That's expensive.
   b) Yes, it is.
   c) Cash or charge?

C. Make questions for the answers.

1. How old _____ ? She's thirteen.
2. _____ ? He's forty-one.
3. _____ ? They're thirteen.
4. Is _____ ? No, he isn't. He's nineteen.
5. _____ ? No, she isn't. She's ten.
6. _____ ? No, it isn't. It's ninety-three.
7. _____ ? She's thirty.

25

VOCABULARY BUILDING

A. Complete the sentences. There are new words here so try your best!

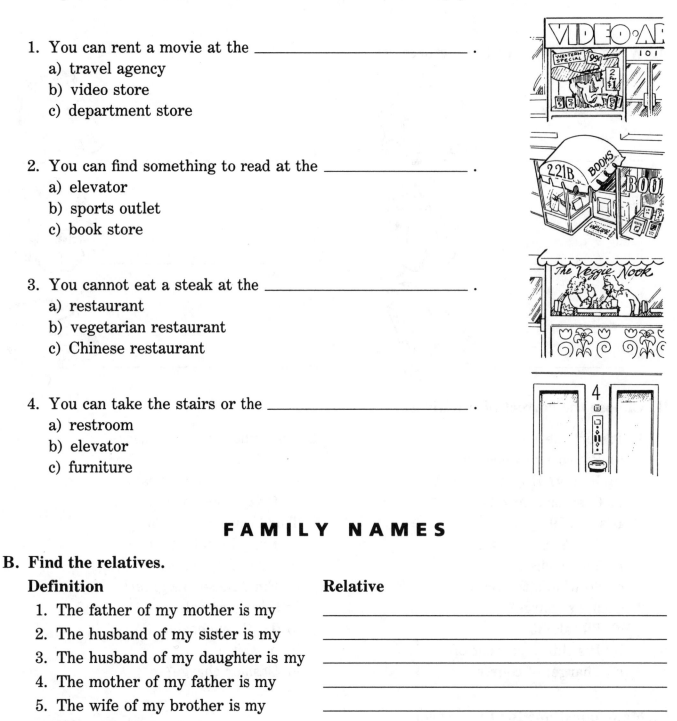

1. You can rent a movie at the _____ .
   a) travel agency
   b) video store
   c) department store

2. You can find something to read at the _____ .
   a) elevator
   b) sports outlet
   c) book store

3. You cannot eat a steak at the _____ .
   a) restaurant
   b) vegetarian restaurant
   c) Chinese restaurant

4. You can take the stairs or the _____ .
   a) restroom
   b) elevator
   c) furniture

FAMILY NAMES

B. Find the relatives.

Definition	Relative
1. The father of my mother is my	_____
2. The husband of my sister is my	_____
3. The husband of my daughter is my	_____
4. The mother of my father is my	_____
5. The wife of my brother is my	_____
6. The wife of my son is my	_____
7. The son of my brother is my	_____
8. The daughter of my sister is my	_____
9. The father of my wife is my	_____
10. The mother of my wife is my	_____
11. The brother of my father is my	_____
12. The sister of my mother is my	_____

CONVERSATION

A. Make a conversation.

You are in the store. They are only two dollars.
You want to buy socks. They are very cheap.
You ask how much they are. You take them and pay cash.

May _____ ?

    Yes, how _____

They _____

    Oh, that's _____

Cash _____ ?

_____

BAY CITY NEWS CROSSWORD

B. Fill in the crossword. Use textbook pages 25–27 for help.

DOWN

1. The average _____ of brides is 20.3.
3. Chris Taylor is a _____ teacher.
4. The band _____ is at 5 p.m.
5. No _____ in the apartment, please
8. 89% of cab drivers are _____ .
9. His wife is dead. he is a _____ .
11. Not the bride.
12. Chris is a college _____ .
13. Buy 3 _____ and get one free!
16. Not married.
20. Children love new _____ .

ACROSS

2. Chris gives classes in her _____ .
6. Chris is a _____ graduate.
7. Boys and girls are _____ .
10. The community _____ is at noon.
14. No longer married.
15. The _____ are at 9 in the evening.
17. Her husband is dead. She is a _____ .
18. New York _____ drivers are from all over.
19. Not female.
21. No _____ needed at Great Hair Cuts!
22. Not the groom.
23. Tony is a part-time _____ .

27

A. Look at the picture of the store. Discuss the store.

B. Read the crossword clues.

DOWN

1. Here's a twenty-dollar bill.
   And here's your _____ . . . $5.00.
2. _____ would be in the Beverages aisle.
4. Where can I find _____ ?
   Aisle 4, Baking Needs.
5. Where can I pay?
   At the _____ .
6. Where can I find _____ cream?
   In aisle 7.
7. Where can I find _____ ?
   In the Bakery, of course.
8. You can find ice _____ in aisle seven.
9. You can find _____ next to milk.
12. Where can I find apples?
    In aisle 6, _____ .
14. Baking Needs are in _____ 4.
19. Goodbye!
    Have a _____ day.

ACROSS

3. Excuse me, where can I find coffee?
   See the sign? _____ ?
5. I have _____ for detergent.
8. You can find corn flakes in _____ , aisle two.
10. I have coupons for _____ .
11. Where can I find sugar for my _____ ?
12. Super _____ World is a supermarket.
13. Where can I find a chicken?
    Try aisle 5, _____ .
15. Where can I find dog food?
    _____ Foods, aisle 1.
16. Where can I find _____ ?
    Aisle 5.
17. You can find _____ next to cheese.
18. Here's a _____-dollar bill.

28

C. Use the picture and the clues. Fill in the crossword puzzle.

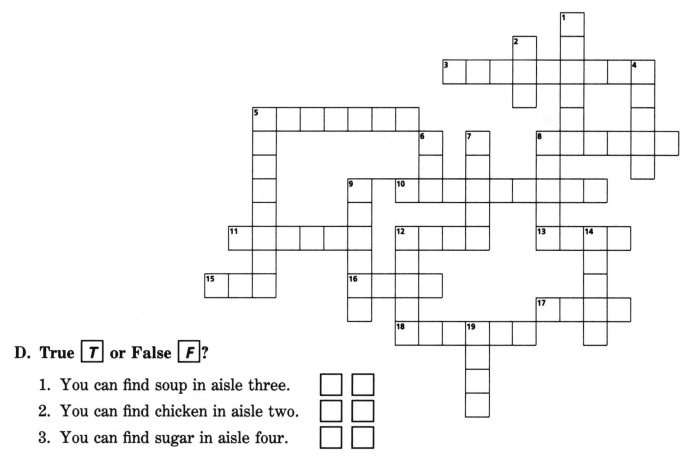

D. True $\boxed{T}$ or False $\boxed{F}$?

1. You can find soup in aisle three.
2. You can find chicken in aisle two.
3. You can find sugar in aisle four.

E. Answer the questions.

1. Where can you find cat food?

   _____

2. Where can you find tea?

   _____

3. Where can you find pears?

   _____

4. Where can you find rolls?

   _____

F. Complete the conversations.

Where can I pay?
   You can pay at _____

How many items do you have?
   I have _____

Okay, go to the _____
   Thanks.

_____

A. Interview a friend.

What is your first name?
What is your last name?
What is your nationality?
Where are you from?
What is your occupation?

My name is Judy.
My last name is Gale.
I am an American.
I am from Miami.
I am an actress.

B. Tell about Judy.

Her first name is Judy.
_____
_____
_____
_____

C. Interview two friends. Write about them.

_____   _____
_____   _____
_____   _____
_____   _____
_____   _____

VOCABULARY BUILDING

an actor

an engineer

an immigration officer

an optician

an umpire

a carpenter

a pharmacist

a plumber

What are their jobs?

Hi! My name is Sue.
I work for the Fixit Company.
I fix bathrooms.

Sue is a plumber.

1. Hi! My name is Marvin.
   I work at the stadium.
   I love baseball!

   _____

2. Hi, my name's Betty.
   I design new malls.
   I work for Buildit Construction.

   _____

3. Hi! My name is Cathy.
   I work in a store.
   I check eyes.

   _____

4. Hi! My name is Jeremy.
   I work at the Mayflower Theater.
   I dance and I sing.

   _____

5. Hi! My name's Ken.
   I work for the government.
   I check passports.

   _____

6. Hi! My name is Hubert.
   I work for Buildit Construction.
   I build houses.

   _____

7. Hi! My name is Peter.
   I work at the pharmacy.
   I fill prescriptions.

   _____

CONVERSATION

A. Complete the conversation.

Ready to order?

_____

Tea or coffee?

_____

With milk, cream, lemon or nothing?

_____

Eggs?

_____

Boiled, fried or scrambled?

_____

Ham, bacon or sausage?

_____

Toast or rolls?

_____

Any juice?

_____

Apple, grapefruit, pineapple or orange?

_____

I'll be right back.

B. Choose the correct alternatives.

1. Ready to order?
   a) What else?
   b) No, not very.
   c) Yes, please.

2. Anything to drink?
   a) Lemon, please.
   b) Ham, please.
   c) Juice, please.

3. Anything else?
   a) No, not very.
   b) Thanks.
   c) A newspaper, please.

C. Make a conversation.

You are in the breakfast room at your motel.
The waitress asks if you are ready to order.
You are very hungry. You order a big breakfast.

Waitress: _____

You: _____

Waitress: _____

You: _____

Waitress: _____

You: _____

VOCABULARY BUILDING

A. Fill in the breakfast order.

```
┌─────────────────────────────────────────────────────┐
│              GOOD MORNING MOTEL                       │
│              Breakfast in your room                   │
│   Time:  6:00–6:15 6:15–6:30 6:30–6:45 6:45–7:00     │
│          7:00–7:15 7:15–7:30 7:30–7:45 7:45–8:00     │
│                                                       │
│   No. of persons:  [1] [2] [3] [4] [5]               │
│   Juice:        orange      tomato    grapefruit      │
│   Number:        ☐            ☐          ☐            │
│                                                       │
│   Eggs:         boiled       fried    scrambled       │
│   Number:        ☐            ☐          ☐            │
│                                                       │
│   Meats:        bacon       sausage     ham           │
│   Number:        ☐            ☐          ☐            │
│                                                       │
│   Cheese:       Dutch        Swiss    American        │
│   Number:        ☐            ☐          ☐            │
│                                                       │
│   Bread:        toast        muffin   sweet roll      │
│   Number:        ☐            ☐          ☐            │
│                                                       │
│   Beverages:   tea with   coffee with black coffee    │
│                  milk        lemon      cream         │
│                  ☐            ☐          ☐            │
│                                                       │
│   All orders include butter, jam, marmalade, sugar.   │
│                                                       │
│   Room number: [  ] Signature: _____         │
│   Print name: _____                 │
└─────────────────────────────────────────────────────┘
```

B. Make a conversation.

It is seven o'clock in the morning.
You are hungry, but where is your breakfast?
Call Room Service and ask about your breakfast.

Room service. Good morning. Can I help you?
  Where _____ ?
What is your room number?

_____ .

And what is your name, please?

_____ .

And what time was your breakfast order?

_____ .

For how many persons?

_____ .

I'll be right with you.

Answer the questions.

What is the dog doing?
It is trying on its new collar. _____

1. What is Tom doing?

_____

2. What are the boys doing?

_____

3. What is Mary doing?

_____

4. What are you doing?

_____

5. What are you two doing?

_____

6. What are the men doing?

_____

7. What are you doing?

_____

8. What is the police officer doing?

_____

VOCABULARY BUILDING

A. Read this.

1. Sidney is on his way to the stadium.

2. Paula is on her way to the market.

3. I am on my way to the train station.

4. We are on our way to the mall.

5. They are on their way to the moon.

6. You are on your way to jail!

7. The dog is on its way to the dog house.

B. Make your own answers.

Where are you going?
  I am going to the mall.
_____

1. Where is Jack going?

_____

2. Where is Maria going?

_____

3. Where are you two going?

_____

4. Where are you going?

_____

5. Where are the boys going?

_____

6. Where is the bus going?

_____

READING COMPREHENSION

A. Read the story.

It is eight o'clock in the evening. Tom is in the bathroom. His father is standing outside the bathroom door. He is knocking on the door.

Come on, Tom!

Just a second! I'm just combing my hair.

It's ten minutes later. His mother and his father are standing outside the bathroom door.

What are you doing in there?

I'm just washing my face.

Well, hurry up!

It's a quarter of an hour later. His mother, father and sister are waiting outside the bathroom door.

Aren't you ready yet?

I'm just brushing my teeth.

It's half past eight. His mother, father, sister and brother are all waiting outside the bathroom door. Tom is finally ready.

Why are you wearing your new shirt?

Why are you wearing your new pants?

Why are you wearing your new shoes?

I'm going out with Sue.

When?

Tomorrow night.

Tomorrow night!

Yes, I'm just trying on everything tonight!

B. Answer the questions.

1. Where is Tom at ten past eight?

_____

2. Where is his mother at half past eight?

_____

3. What is his father doing at eight o'clock?

_____

4. Where are his mother and father at half past eight?

_____

5. When is Tom going out with Sue?

_____

6. Why is he wearing his new clothes?

_____

REVIEW
VOCABULARY

A. Write the words for the pictures.

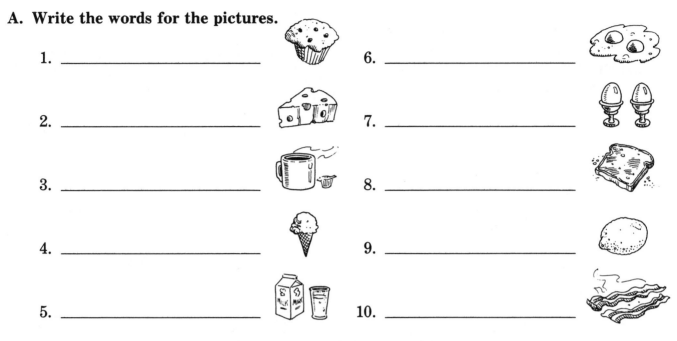

1. _____

2. _____

3. _____

4. _____

5. _____

6. _____

7. _____

8. _____

9. _____

10. _____

CONVERSATION

B. Choose the correct alternative.

1. Juice?
   a) Yes, orange juice, please.
   b) Sunny side up, please.
   c) Waffles, please.

2. Coffee?
   a) Yes, thanks. With cream, please.
   b) Yes, please. With lemon.
   c) Yes, pancakes.

3. Eggs?
   a) Yes, please. Scrambled.
   b) No coffee, thank you.
   c) Yes, a muffin, please.

4. Bread?
   a) Ham and sausage, please.
   b) Toast and a sweet roll, please.
   c) Grapefruit, please.

C. What are they doing?

1. _He is combing his hair._ _____

2. _____

3. _____

4. _____

5. _____

6. _____

VOCABULARY BUILDING

A. Complete the sentences. There are new words here so try your best!

1. The worker is in the _____.
   a) hospital
   b) factory
   c) store

2. The teacher is in the _____.
   a) city hall
   b) station
   c) school

3. The attendant is in the _____.
   a) airplane
   b) hospital
   c) market

4. The sales clerk is in the _____.
   a) community center
   b) store
   c) motel

5. The programmer is in the _____.
   a) restaurant
   b) fire station
   c) computer room

CONVERSATION

B. Make a conversation.

You are in a coffee shop.
It is 2 o'clock in the afternoon.
You are not very hungry but you are very thirsty.
The waitress asks you if you are ready to order.

Waitress: _____

You: _____

Waitress: _____

You: _____

Waitress: _____

You: _____

Waitress: _____

You: _____

BAY CITY NEWS CROSSWORD

Fill in the crossword puzzle. Use textbook pages 37–39.

DOWN

2. The Bake Sale is on Saturday. The _____ date is Sunday.
4. Auto Parts is an _____ company.
5. The _____ of API is auto parts.
6. Dollars and cents.
7. The workers work in the _____ .
9. I like orange _____ .
12. API is looking for _____ mechanics.
13. Saturdays and Sundays.
15. The Flea _____ is very popular.
16. The _____ market is on the weekend.
18. The Air Force gives you free _____ care.
20. Sunlight shining through water vapor.
21. I want a hot _____.
25. Not the bottom.

ACROSS

1. Sixty minutes.
3. Not husband.
8. API's business is _____ parts.
10. The _____ Park is expanding.
11. Boys and girls.
14. My father is a factory _____ .
17. Bay _____ is a nice place to live.
19. Money from the Bake Sale goes to the _____ .
22. Sloan's Supermarket wants cashiers for weekends _____ .
23. Free medical and _____ care.
24. The Industrial Park is _____ , getting bigger.
26. The _____ is $5 an hour.
27. The _____ from the sale go to the library.
28. Not the top.

UNIT 4

A. Look at the picture of the house. Discuss the house.

B. Read the crossword clues.

DOWN

1. Where are the _____ ?
   They're in the hall.
2. Where is the table?
   It's in the _____ .
3. Where's the TV?
   It's in the _____ room.
5. Where's my bike?
   It's in the _____ .
6. Where are the _____ ?
   They're in the kitchen.
7. Where's the cat?
   _____ is in the kitchen.
8. Where's the piano?
   It's in the _____ .
11. Where are the dishes?
    They are in the _____ .
13. Where are the towels?
    They are in the _____ .
15. Where is my _____ ?
    It is in the bathroom, of course.
16. Where are the _____ ?
    They are with the pots.

ACROSS

4. What's Mother doing?
   She is _____ the lamps.
6. Where's the dog?
   It's in the _____ room.
9. Mother is unpacking the _____ .
10. Where's the bookcase?
    It's in the _____ .
12. Where's my bed?
    In your _____ , of course!
14. Where are the _____ ?
    They are in the bedroom.
16. Where are the _____ and pans?
17. The _____ are on the table in the yard.
18. The _____ are in a box on the piano in the basement.

40

C. Use the picture and the clues. Fill in the crossword puzzle.

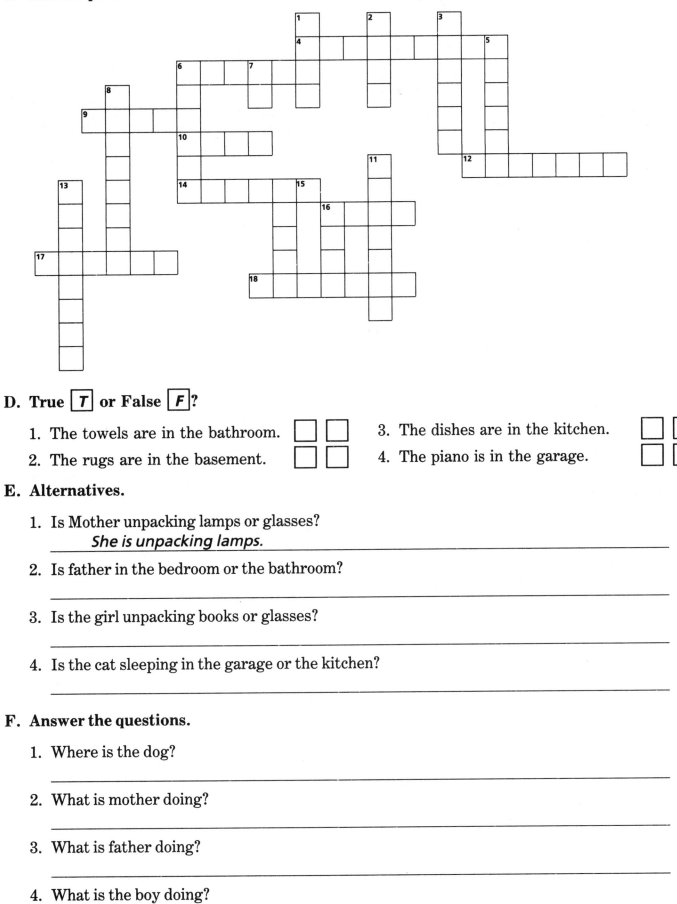

D. True `T` **or False** `F`?

1. The towels are in the bathroom. ☐ ☐
2. The rugs are in the basement. ☐ ☐

3. The dishes are in the kitchen. ☐ ☐
4. The piano is in the garage. ☐ ☐

E. Alternatives.

1. Is Mother unpacking lamps or glasses?
   She is unpacking lamps.

2. Is father in the bedroom or the bathroom?
   _____

3. Is the girl unpacking books or glasses?
   _____

4. Is the cat sleeping in the garage or the kitchen?
   _____

F. Answer the questions.

1. Where is the dog?
   _____

2. What is mother doing?
   _____

3. What is father doing?
   _____

4. What is the boy doing?
   _____

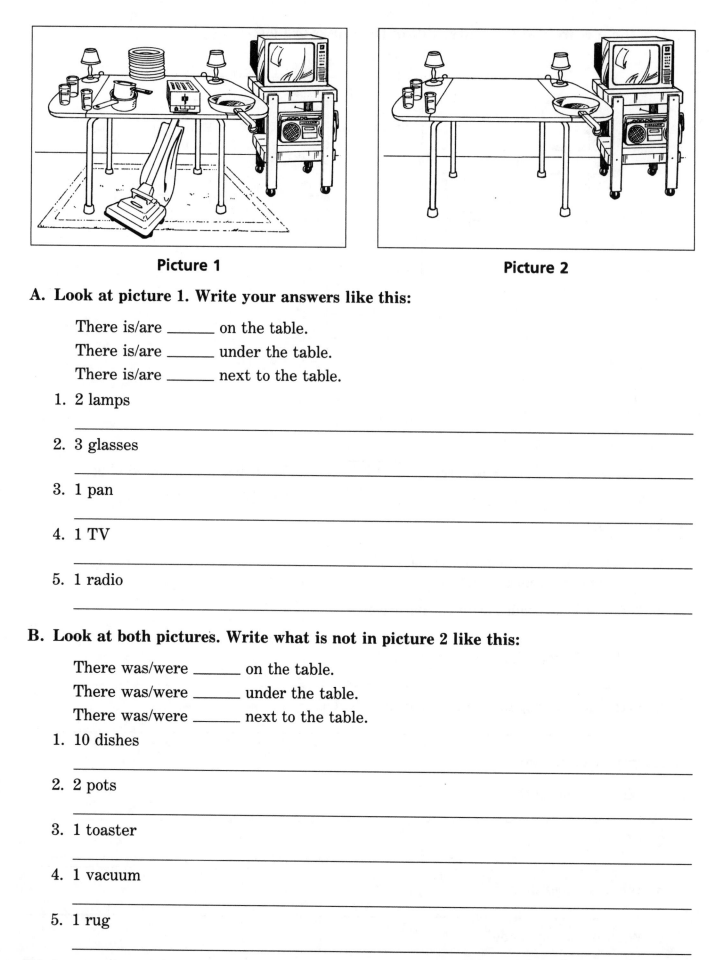

Picture 1   **Picture 2**

A. Look at picture 1. Write your answers like this:

There is/are _____ on the table.

There is/are _____ under the table.

There is/are _____ next to the table.

1. 2 lamps

_____

2. 3 glasses

_____

3. 1 pan

_____

4. 1 TV

_____

5. 1 radio

_____

B. Look at both pictures. Write what is not in picture 2 like this:

There was/were _____ on the table.

There was/were _____ under the table.

There was/were _____ next to the table.

1. 10 dishes

_____

2. 2 pots

_____

3. 1 toaster

_____

4. 1 vacuum

_____

5. 1 rug

_____

VOCABULARY BUILDING

A. Look at this weather chart for next week. The weather is very changeable.

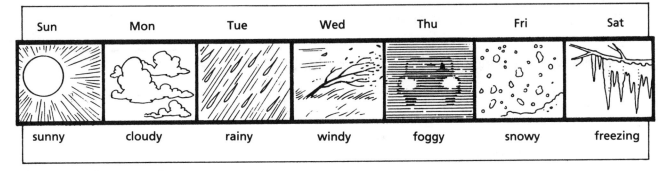

Sun	Mon	Tue	Wed	Thu	Fri	Sat
sunny	cloudy	rainy	windy	foggy	snowy	freezing

B. Answer the questions.

What day is it today?

1. It is rainy. _Tuesday_

2. It is snowy. _____

3. It is cloudy. _____

What day is it today?

4. It was sunny yesterday. _____

5. It was foggy yesterday. _____

6. It was windy yesterday. _____

What day is it today?

7. It will be freezing tomorrow.

_____

8. It will be windy tomorrow.

_____

9. It will be snowy tomorrow.

_____

What day is it today?

10. It will be sunny the day after tomorrow.

_____

11. It will be rainy the day after tomorrow.

_____

12. It will be foggy the day after tomorrow.

_____

What day is it today?

13. It was freezing the day before yesterday.

_____

14. It was cloudy the day before yesterday.

_____

15. It was windy the day before yesterday.

_____

C. Look at the weather chart again. Answer the questions.

1. What day is it today?

_____

2. What's the weather like?

_____

3. What was the weather like yesterday?

_____

4. What will the weather be like tomorrow?

_____

5. What was the weather like the day before yesterday?

_____

CONVERSATION

A. Complete the conversation. The sweater is the wrong size.

Can I help you? What's the problem?

_____

Of course we'll exchange it. What's wrong with it?

_____

What size is it?

_____

And what size do you want?

_____

That's fine. We'll exchange it.

B. Complete the conversation. The dishes are broken.

What's the problem?

_____

What's wrong with them?

_____

Are they broken? Really?

_____

Do you want to return them or exchange them?

_____

Certainly. We'll exchange them for you.

C. Answer the questions.

1. What is wrong with these sheets?

_____

2. What is wrong with this vase?

_____

3. What is wrong with these pants?

_____

4. What is wrong with this toaster?

_____

5. What is wrong with this sweater?

_____

6. What is wrong with these glasses?

_____

VOCABULARY BUILDING

A. Read these ads.

HOUSES FOR SALE

2 bedroom, 1 bath, kitchen, living room, 1 story, downtown. Call 908-3852, evenings after 6:00.

1 bedroom/living room, small kitchen, bathroom, on the beach. Call 693-8910, day or night.

5 bedroom, 3 bathroom, living room, den, large kitchen, garage in basement, 5 miles from downtown. Call: 402-8975, 9 a.m. to 5 p.m.

3 bedroom, 1 bathroom, kitchen, living room, large basement, garage, large yard, on a lake, 45 miles from downtown. Call 491-8933 (office hours) or 539-7739 (after 8 p.m.)

B. Answer the questions.

What number would you call if

1. you wanted a house with five bedrooms?
   I would call _____

2. you wanted a house with two bedrooms?
   _____

3. you wanted a house with only one story?
   _____

4. you wanted a house with a den?
   _____

5. you wanted a house downtown?
   _____

C. Write your own ad.

_____
_____
_____
_____

VOCABULARY BUILDING

A. Look at these people.

Tania is tall.
Mark is short.

Chris is tall and thin.
Karl is short and fat.

Lena is short and slim.
Bud is tall and chubby.

Carol is slim and of medium height.
Joe is tall and of medium build.

Sue   Jack   Jane   Ken   Pete

Sue has long, straight hair.
Jack has short, curly hair.

Jane has long wavy hair.
Ken is thin on top.
Pete is bald.

B. Answer the questions.

Who is tall?
  Joe is./Joe and Bud are.

Who has long hair?
  Sue has./Sue and Jane have.

1. Who is short?

2. Who is slim?

3. Who has short hair?

4. Who is bald?

5. Who is fat?

6. Who is chubby?

7. Who has wavy hair?

8. Who is of medium build?

A. Fill in the missing words.

1. I am going to fix my roof.
   John is going to help ____me____ .

2. Mary is going to paint her garage.
   Tom is going to help _____ .

3. Peter is going to clean out his basement.
   I am going to help _____ .

4. We are going to weed our garden.
   Ken is going to help _____ .

5. If you are going to wash your car, I am going to help _____ .

6. If you two are going to mow the lawn, I am not going to help _____ .

B. Write sentences. Follow the example.

Where are you going?
I am going to the garage.
_____

What are you going to do there?
I am going to get my bike.
_____

1. Where are you going?
   _____

   What are you going to do there?
   _____

2. Where are you going?
   _____

   What are you going to do there?
   _____

3. Where are you going?
   _____

   What are you going to do there?
   _____

4. Where are you going?
   _____

   What are you going to do there?
   _____

READING COMPREHENSION

A. Read the story.

Mary's Vacation

Mary is on vacation. She is on her way to Arizona. She is going to visit her friend, Herman. Herman is going to fix up his rusty old motorbike, and Mary is going to help him.

Next week, Mary and Herman are going for a trip on the bike. They are going to make their way to the west coast for the first two or three days.

Then they are going to a lake in the mountains for the rest of the week. They hope the weather is going to be good. They are going to sleep in a very small tent.

B. Answer the questions.

1. Why isn't Mary going to work next week?

   _____

2. Why is she going to Arizona?

   _____

3. Why are Herman and Mary going to fix up the motorbike?

   _____

4. Where are they going first?

   _____

5. How long are they going to stay on the coast?

   _____

6. Where are they going after the first two or three days?

   _____

7. Where are they going to sleep?

   _____

REVIEW
VOCABULARY

A. Write the words for the pictures.

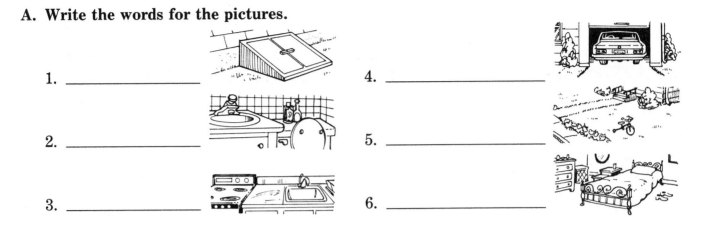

1. _____

2. _____

3. _____

4. _____

5. _____

6. _____

CONVERSATION

B. Choose the correct alternatives.

1. I'd like to return this radio.
   a) What's the problem?
   b) Can I help you?
   c) They're torn.

2. What's wrong with it?
   a) They're torn.
   b) It's torn.
   c) It's damaged.

3. Is it too big?
   a) Yes, it's the wrong size.
   b) Yes, they're dirty.
   c) Yes, it's the wrong color.

4. What's wrong with the dish?
   a) It's cracked.
   b) They're dirty.
   c) It's torn.

5. What was the weather like today?
   a) It was cold.
   b) It will be cold.
   c) It is cold.

6. What's the weather like today?
   a) It's hot.
   b) It was hot.
   c) It'll be hot.

7. What will it be like tomorrow?
   a) It was wet.
   a) It will be wet.
   c) It is wet?

8. What was it like yesterday?
   a) It was dry.
   a) It will be dry.
   b) It is dry.

C. What's the weather like?

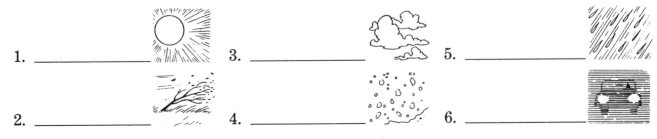

1. _____

2. _____

3. _____

4. _____

5. _____

6. _____

VOCABULARY BUILDING

A. Complete the sentences. There are new words here so try your best!

1. The towel goes in the _____.
   a) bathroom   b) garage   c) yard

2. The toaster goes in the _____.
   a) bathroom   b) den   c) kitchen

3. The sheet goes in the _____.
   a) bedroom   b) attic   c) yard

4. The bike goes in the _____.
   a) garage   b) yard   c) den

5. The dog sleeps in the _____.
   a) bathroom   b) bedroom   c) dog house

6. The cat sleeps in the _____.
   a) bathtub   b) basket   c) pan

CONVERSATION

B. Make a conversation.

You are in a store.
You want to return a book.
The clerk asks you what is wrong.
The book is torn.
The clerk asks if you want to return the book or exchange it.
You exchange it for a new book.

Clerk: _____

You: _____

Clerk: _____

You: _____

Clerk: _____

You: _____

BAY CITY NEWS CROSSWORD

Fill in the crossword puzzle. Use textbook pages 49–51 for help.

DOWN

1. The first thing you eat in the morning.
2. Put it in the refrigerator, not in the _____ .
3. Not wet.
4. Their music is very _____ .
6. The coach _____ to the mountains are popular.
8. They raise money for the _____ .
9. Before October.
10. 7% of the Earth's land _____ is in the temperate zone.
12. My cat sleeps on my _____ .
13. After Thursday.

ACROSS

5. The _____ in the coach are comfortable.
7. Put it in the _____ , not in the freezer.
8. There are 24 _____ in a day.
11. Let's go to the Flea _____ .
13. The _____ is for the Homeless Shelter.
14. The _____ Market is on Friday and Saturday.
15. I drive a _____ , not a car.
16. Not day.
17. I go to work by _____ .
18. After summer but before winter.
19. Bake a cake in the _____ .

UNIT 5

A. Look at the picture of the neighborhood. Discuss the neighborhood.

B. Read the crossword clues.

DOWN

1. What are you _____ ?
2. I am _____ the trash.
4. John is _____ fish for lunch.
5. Henry is washing his _____ .
6. The cat is _____ under the table.
8. John is going to cook _____ , too.
11. Henry is _____ his shirts.
14. Sally is _____ the bathroom.
    She is sweeping the floor.
15. Karen is _____ the sheets.
16. Peter _____ in town yesterday.
20. Where _____ the children yesterday?
21. Mike is scrubbing the _____ .

ACROSS

3. Sally is _____ the floor.
7. Henry is doing the _____ .
9. Where _____ you yesterday?
10. John is in the _____ .
12. Where were you yesterday?
    I _____ in town.
13. Jane is _____ her bed.
14. The _____ is in the garage.
17. I am emptying the _____ .
18. Sally is sweeping the floor in the _____ .
19. Henry is _____ his clothes.
22. Please open the _____ . It is very hot.
23. Mike is _____ the tub.

C. Use the picture and the clues. Fill in the crossword puzzle.

D. Answer the questions.

1. What was Henry doing?

_____

2. What was Mike doing?

_____

3. What was John doing?

_____

4. What was Karen doing?

_____

5. What was Jane doing?

_____

6. What was Sally doing?

_____

7. Where was Peter yesterday?

_____

8. What were the cat and the dog doing?

_____

9. What were the children doing?

_____

Discuss the pictures. Then make questions and answers. Use any names you like.

Where was Peter at five o'clock yesterday?
He was at the bike shop. He was buying a bike.

1. _____
_____
_____

2. _____
_____
_____

3. _____
_____
_____

4. _____
_____
_____

5. _____
_____
_____

6. _____
_____
_____

Discuss the pictures. Then make questions and answers. Use any names you like.

Where were Sally and Lucy at nine o'clock yesterday evening?

They were at home. They were watching TV.

_____

1. _____
   _____
   _____

2. _____
   _____
   _____

3. _____
   _____
   _____

4. _____
   _____
   _____

5. _____
   _____
   _____

6. _____
   _____
   _____

CONVERSATION

A. Complete the conversation.

May I help you?

_____

Where do you want to go?

_____

When do you want to go?

_____

How do you want to go?

_____

Okay. Departures are on Wednesdays and Saturdays.

_____

For 6 nights, 10 nights, or 14 nights?

_____

Here are some brochures.

_____

You're welcome.

B. Fill in the names of the months. One month is missing.

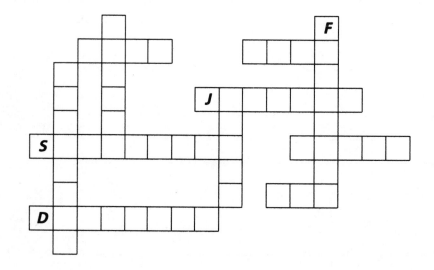

The missing month is

_____

VOCABULARY BUILDING

Answer the questions.

Where was Mary yesterday?
She was at the Hardware Store.

What was she doing?
She was buying a shovel.

1. Where was Harry the day before yesterday?

What was he doing?

2. Where were Kate and Sue last Monday?

What were they doing?

3. Where were Tim and Tom last night?

What were they doing?

4. Where was Jack yesterday evening?

What was he doing?

5. Where was Jill a minute ago?

What was she doing?

VOCABULARY BUILDING

A. Make conversations like this.

Where's **the United States?**
   It's **north of Mexico.**
Below **Canada?**
   Yes, it is **south of Canada.**

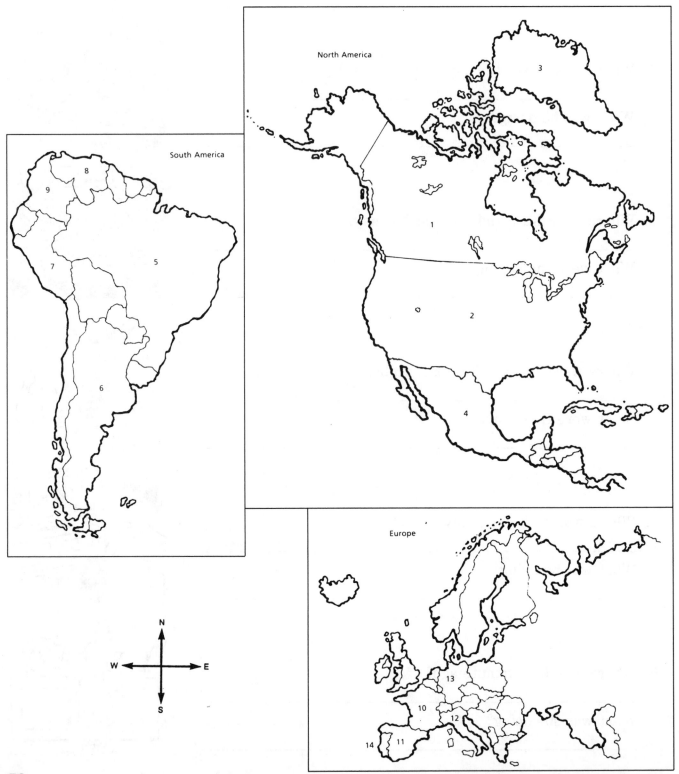

B. How many countries can you name?

North America

1. _____
2. _____
3. _____
4. _____

South America

5. _____
6. _____
7. _____
8. _____
9. _____

Europe

10. _____
11. _____
12. _____
13. _____
14. _____

Africa

15. _____
16. _____
17. _____

Asia

18. _____
19. _____
20. _____
21. _____
22. _____

Australia

23. _____
24. _____

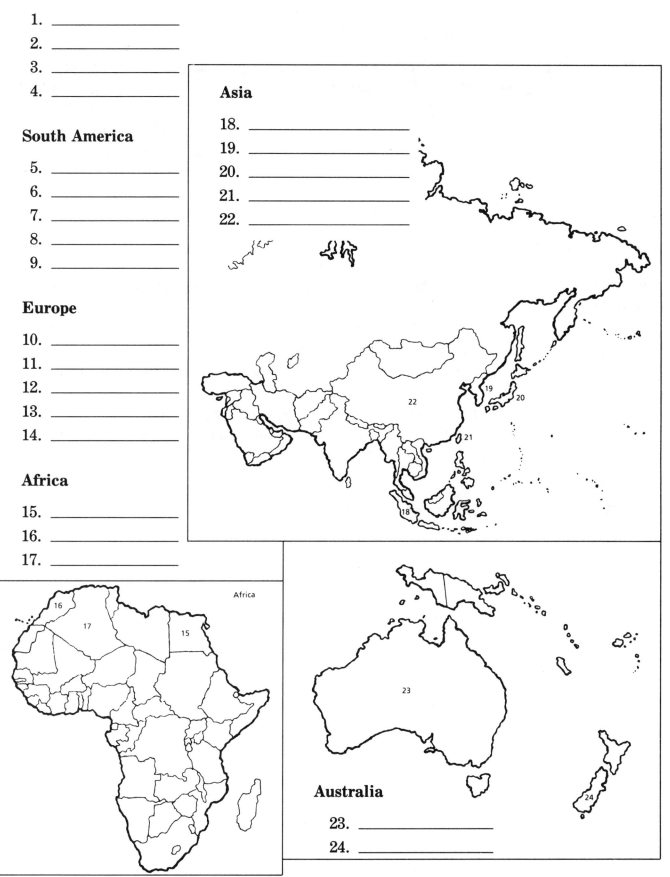

Africa

READING COMPREHENSION

A. Read the story.

Our Vacation

A month ago, my friends and I were on vacation. We were on a small island. We are all very interested in diving, fishing, swimming and sailing.

We were very lucky. The weather was fine. It was not windy, but there was a nice breeze from the ocean. So it was not too hot and not too cold.

It was sunny most of the time. But every day, at about two o'clock in the afternoon, there was a short shower. So it was not too wet and not too dry.

The hotel was very nice. It was not too big and not too small. There were about fifty rooms.

The hotel was not crowded. It was not full and it was not empty. There were about thirty guests for breakfast every morning and about twenty guests for dinner every evening.

B. Answer the questions.

1. When were they on vacation?

   _____

2. Why were they on an island?

   _____

3. Why was it not too hot?

   _____

4. Why was it not too cold?

   _____

5. Why was it not too dry?

   _____

6. Why was it not too wet?

   _____

7. Why was the hotel not too crowded?

   _____

REVIEW
VOCABULARY

A. Write the words for the pictures.

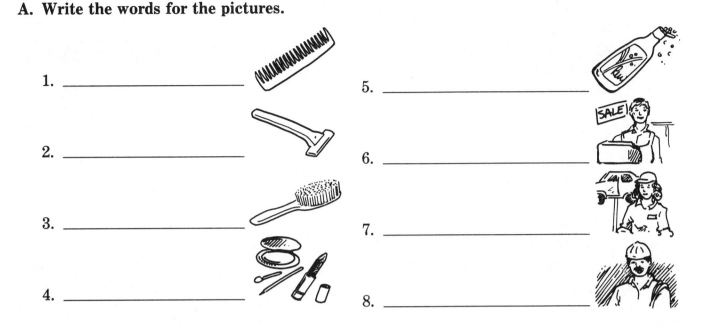

1. _____

2. _____

3. _____

4. _____

5. _____

6. _____

7. _____

8. _____

CONVERSATION

B. Choose the correct alternatives.

1. Where do you want to go?
   a) In June.
   b) By bus.
   c) To California.

2. How do you want to go?
   a) By boat.
   b) In May.
   c) Thank you.

3. When do you want to go?
   a) By car.
   b) To Japan.
   c) In August.

4. Here are some brochures.
   a) You're welcome.
   b) I'll return it.
   c) Thanks.

QUESTIONS

C. What were they doing yesterday?

1. What was Ken doing?

   _____

2. What was Sally doing?

   _____

3. What was Jack doing?

   _____

4. What were the dogs doing?

   _____

VOCABULARY BUILDING

A. Complete the sentences. There are new words here so try your best!

1. The cashier is on her way to the _____.
   a) checkout
   b) garage
   c) basement

2. The officers are on their way to the _____.
   a) attic
   b) police station
   c) yard

3. The mechanic is on her way to the _____.
   a) garage
   b) magazine
   c) supermarket

4. The x-ray technician is on his way to the _____.
   a) laboratory
   b) basement
   c) attic

5. The construction workers are on their way to the _____.
   a) site
   b) office
   c) makeup

B. Fill in the names of the continents.

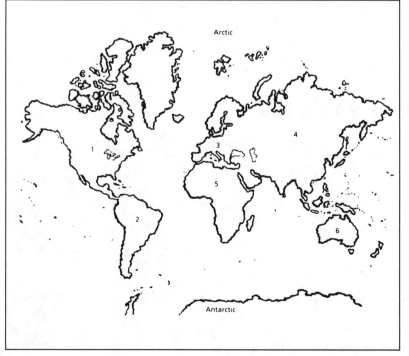

1. _____

2. _____

3. _____

4. _____

5. _____

6. _____

BAY CITY NEWS CROSSWORD

Fill in the crossword puzzle. Use textbook pages 61–63 for help.

DOWN

1.
3. They are getting _____ in December.
4. The doctor is with a _____ .
5. This is a hospital for the _____ .
6. Anne made a _____ quilt.
8. This warms the _____ .
9. This _____ is for the elderly.
13. Give me some tips on how to _____ .

ACROSS

2. Dan and Jane announce their _____ .
4. I read my books at the _____ library.
7. The _____ examined my sick dog.
8. They do this in _____ of their friends.
9. This is a _____ quilt.
10. Not short.
11. The doctor is talking to the _____ about a patient.
12. The _____ of the hospital for the elderly are all over 60.
14. Not my son.
15. She has a handmade _____ .
16. She gives them _____ tips on how to study.

UNIT 6

A. Look at the picture of the laundromat. Discuss the laundromat.

B. Read the crossword clues.

DOWN

1. The woman has a _____ in her right hand.
2. The boy is emptying the _____ .
3. The dog is pulling the _____ .
4. The boy has a _____ bag.
6. The boy is putting his shirt in a _____ .
8. My laundry, please.
   Where is your _____ ?
   Here you are.
9. The boy is wearing a _____ .
11. The woman has a purse in her right _____ .
13. The woman is wearing a _____ .
14. Blanket/Bedspread/_____/Special.
16. The boy is putting his _____ in a bag.
17. The man is wearing a business _____ .
23. The _____ machine is next to the door.

ACROSS

5. The woman has an _____ in her left hand.
7. The dog is pulling the blanket out of the _____ .
10. There is a _____ on the umbrella.
12. I don't have my receipt.
    What was the _____ ?
    A nightgown.
15. The dog is standing in a _____ .
18. A _____ is talking with the cashier.
19. A bottle of _____ is on the washer.
20. The business man is holding an _____ .
21. The girl is wearing a _____ .
22. The customer at the counter is wearing a _____ .
24. A _____ special is $6.99.
25. The _____ dress is on the counter.

C. Use the picture and the clues. Fill in the crossword puzzle.

D. Answer the questions.

1. What is the man wearing?

_____

2. What is the boy wearing?

_____

3. What is the woman with the purse wearing?

_____

4. What is the girl wearing?

_____

5. What is the man doing?

_____

6. What is the girl doing?

_____

7. What is the woman at the counter doing?

_____

8. What is the dog doing?

_____

A. Answer the questions.

Do they like basketball?
No, they don't. They like baseball.

1. Do Tom and Betty like karate?

   _____

2. Do Mary and Jane like spaghetti?

   _____

3. Do the children like bananas?

   _____

4. Do their parents like wrestling?

   _____

5. Do the dogs like eggs?

   _____

B. Make questions. Use any names you like.

1. _____

   No, they don't like spaghetti. They like rice.

2. _____

   No, they don't play golf. They play tennis.

3. _____

   No, I don't like boxing. I like wrestling.

4. _____

   No, we don't like candy. We like fruit.

5. _____

   No, they don't play football. They play baseball.

VOCABULARY BUILDING

A. Read the conversations.

Do you like **cats?**
  Yes, I do. Do you like **cats?**
Yes, I do.

Do you like **cats?**
  No, I don't, but I like **dogs.** Do you
  like **dogs?**
Yes, I do.

or

No, I don't, but I like **rabbits.** Do you like
rabbits?

B. Make new conversations.

Animals

1. rabbits   2. pigs   3. cows   4. horses   5. dogs   6. birds

Meat and Seafood

1. ham   2. beef   3. veal   4. pork   5. chicken

6. turkey   7. lobster   8. sole   9. shrimp

Fruits

1. oranges   2. apples   3. grapes   4. bananas   5. cherries   6. pears

Vegetables

1. carrots   2. potatoes   3. peas   4. beans   5. cucumber   6. tomatoes

CONVERSATION

A. Complete the conversation.

Can I help you?

_____

This green one?

_____

Oh, yes. That one.

_____

It's extra large.

_____

Is this one better?

_____

It's forty-nine dollars.

_____

Cash or charge?

_____

B. Choose the correct alternative.

1. Need some help?
   a) Yes, they are.
   b) Yes, it is.
   c) Yes, please.
2. How do they look?
   a) It looks nice.
   b) Yes, they are.
   c) Nice.

3. Can I try them on?
   a) I'll take it.
   b) I'll take them.
   c) Certainly.
4. Are those size eight?
   a) No, they're not.
   b) Yes, it is.
   c) This is.

C. Make a conversation.

There is a sale at the Sports Outlet.
Not all shorts are on sale.
You ask for shorts on sale.

You want a medium size.
You want to try them on.
They are not cheap but you take them.

Clerk: _____

You: _____

Clerk: _____

You: _____

Clerk: _____

You: _____

Clerk: _____

You: _____

VOCABULARY BUILDING

A. Make new conversations like this.

Clothing Styles

Do you like this dress?
   I don't really like **striped** clothes.

1. striped

2. checked

3. polka-dot

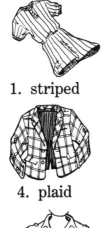

4. plaid

5. flowered

6. paisley

7. baggy

8. tight

9. loose

Footwear

Do you like these **high heels?**
   I prefer **flats.**

1. high heels

2. flats

3. running shoes

4. sandals

5. slippers

6. loafers

7. sneakers

8. boots

9. cowboy boots

VOCABULARY BUILDING

A. Look at these household jobs.

1. dusting

2. feeding pets

3. sweeping floors

4. washing dishes

5. drying dishes

6. cleaning windows

7. vacuum cleaning

8. making beds

9. tidying up

10. painting

11. fixing things

12. wallpapering

13. doing the laundry

14. mowing the lawn

15. ironing

16. watering plants

17. emptying trash

18. cooking meals

B. Interview your friends like this.

Do you like **washing dishes?**
    Yes, I do. I always/often do it.
                or
    No, I don't. I never/seldom do it.

C. What about you? Fill in the poll.

The Good Housekeeper Poll

	Always	Often	Sometimes	Seldom	Never
1. Dusting					
2. Feeding pets					
3. Sweeping floors					
4. Drying dishes					
5. Washing dishes					
6. Cleaning windows					
7. Vacuum cleaning					
8. Making beds					
9. Tidying up					
10. Painting					
11. Fixing things					
12. Wallpapering					
13. Doing the laundry					
14. Mowing the lawn					
15. Ironing					
16. Watering flowers					
17. Emptying trash					
18. Cooking meals					

D. Write about what you do.

I sometimes _____

I never _____

I often _____

I always _____

READING COMPREHENSION

A. Read the story.

The Terrible Twins

My sister and her husband have two children. Thank goodness they don't have more than two! We call them the Terrible Twins!

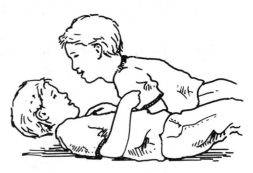

They don't listen to their parents. They do exactly what they want.

They don't go to bed early. They go to bed very late. They never go to bed before eleven o'clock in the evening!

But they don't get up late. They get up very early every day! They always get up before six o'clock in the morning!

But do they go to school on time? No, they do not! They never have their breakfast in the kitchen. They sit in the living room and watch television. They don't watch the morning news. They watch MTV! They are always late for school.

After school they do not come straight home. They play with their friends. In the evening, they don't do their homework. They sit in front of the television again and watch videos.

But, as my sister and her husband say, "You are only young once!"

B. Answer the questions.

1. How many children do my sister and her husband have?

   _____

2. Are they the same age or are they different ages?

   _____

3. When do they go to bed?

   _____

4. When do they get up?

   _____

5. Where do they have breakfast?

   _____

6. Why?

   _____

7. Why are they always late for school?

   _____

8. What do they do after school?

   _____

REVIEW
VOCABULARY

A. Write the words for the pictures.

1. _____

2. _____

3. _____

4. _____

5. _____

6. _____

7. _____

8. _____

9. _____

10. _____

CONVERSATION

B. Choose the correct alternatives.

1. Is that gold?
   a) Yes, they are.
   b) No, they aren't.
   c) Yes, it is.
2. Those are on special offer?
   a) That's why they're cheap.
   b) That's why it's expensive.
   c) Certainly.
3. How much is that?
   a) Those are $60.
   b) They are $60.
   c) It's $60.
4. How do they look?
   a) Certainly.
   b) Try it on.
   c) Very nice.

C. Write about your housekeeping. Use these words.

1. seldom

   _____

2. never

   _____

3. sometimes

   _____

4. always

   _____

VOCABULARY BUILDING

A. Choose the correct alternative. There are new words here so try your best!

1. The day care worker is on her way to the _____.
   a) restaurant
   b) Day Care Center
   c) laundromat

2. The veterinarian is on her way to the _____.
   a) clinic
   b) store
   c) library

3. The programmer is on his way to the _____.
   a) florist
   b) bank
   c) computer lab

4. The seamstress is at the _____.
   a) computer
   b) sewing machine
   c) sink

5. The butcher is at the _____.
   a) bank
   b) night club
   c) Butcher shop

6. The farmer is at the _____.
   a) grocery store
   b) farm
   c) mall

CONVERSATION

B. Make a conversation.

You see a pair of jeans on special.
You ask how much they are.
You ask if they have your size.

You want to try them on.
You ask how you look.
You look great.

You: _____

Clerk: _____

You: _____

Clerk: _____

You: _____

Clerk: _____

You: _____

Clerk: _____

BAY CITY NEWS CROSSWORD

Fill in the crossword puzzle. Use textbook pages 73–75 for help.

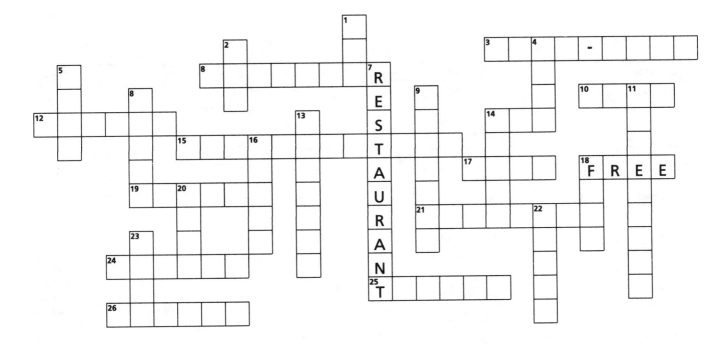

DOWN

1. She is eating a turkey _____ .
2. A _____ of soda, please.
4. 12 o'clock.
5. The shoes are cheap because they are on _____ .
7. Let's eat in the _____ .
8. They announced the _____ of their daughter.
9. Not afternoon.
11. Appointments are not _____ for the Blood Pressure Clinic.
13. The planes land at the _____ .
14. The police arrive on the _____ .
16. Not late.
18. The police are investigating the _____ .
20. The restaurant is _____ to the hangar.
22. Check your _____ pressure!
23. Not female.

ACROSS

3. The Seaside _____ has weekly specials.
6. Not my son.
10. This house is for _____ .
12. The hospital has a new Blood Pressure _____ .
14. Not my daughter.
15. The _____ soon arrive on the scene.
17. _____ wanted.
18. The clinic is _____ . You don't pay.
19. The fire was in the large _____ .
21. After October but before December.
24. Help _____ .
25. She is eating a _____ pie.
26. Not male.

75

UNIT 7

A. Look at the picture of the restaurant. Discuss the restaurant.

B. Read the crossword clues.

DOWN

1. _____ sandwich or chicken sandwich?
2. Ready to order?
   No, may I have a _____ , please?
3. Fish sandwich or _____ sandwich?
6. Ketchup and _____
7. You have ketchup on your shirt.
   Oh, give me some _____ .
8. I like _____ on my French Fries.
11. A chicken _____ , please.
12. Apple _____ or ice cream?
14. I like sugar in my _____ .
16. Something to drink?
   Yes, a small _____ , please.
21. A _____ of apple pie, please.
22. They are drinking juice through _____ .
23. I like _____ pie.
25. I need some sweetner for my _____ .
26. I like _____ rings with my hamburger.
28. Juice or _____ ?
30. A large pizza to _____ , please.
31. Something to _____ ?
32. I like _____ and sugar in my coffee.
33. A _____ or a cheeseburger?
36. A menu, _____ .
38. I like an ice cream _____ .
40. I like _____ cheese on my pizza.

ACROSS

1. _____ Fries or potatoes.
3. Hamburger or _____ ?
4. French _____ or potatoes?
5. Small, _____ or large?
9. I like _____ in my coffee.
10. I'll have a chicken _____ sandwich.
13. That's not sugar. It's _____ .
15. Apple pie or _____ cream?
17. I like _____ on my hamburger.
18. Something _____ drink?
19. A slice of _____ , please.
20. Small, medium or _____ ?
22. Large, medium or _____ ?
24. _____ and mustard?
27. Sugar or _____ ?
29. I like _____ juice.
34. I like apple and orange _____ .
35. I like onion _____ with my cheeseburger.
37. Here you are.
   _____ .
39. I like to drink _____ .
41. I like to drink _____ water.

C. Use the picture and the clues. Fill in the crossword puzzle.

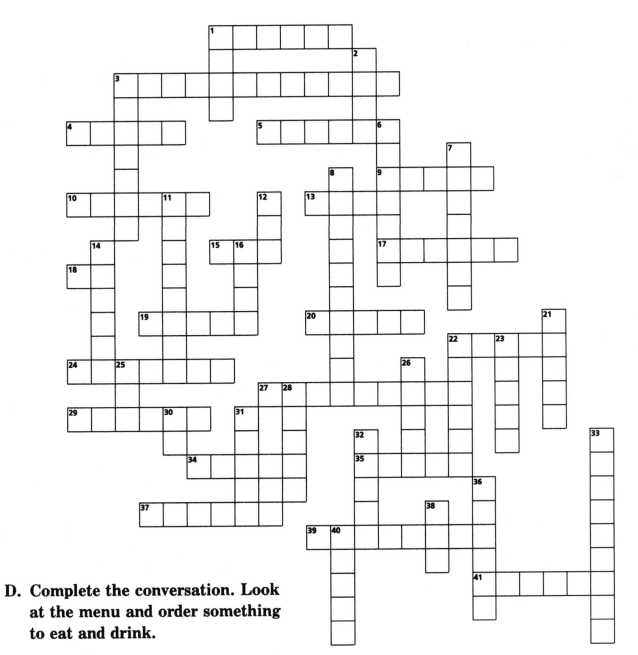

D. Complete the conversation. Look at the menu and order something to eat and drink.

Can I help you? Something to eat?

_____

Something to drink?

_____

Anything else?

_____

They are over there. Is that all?

_____

It's over there. Is that it?

_____

That's _____ , please.

A. Look at this timetable.

DESTINATION	DEPARTURE	ARRIVAL	TRACK	ONE WAY	ROUND-TRIP
Seattle	8:00	9:15	5	$15	$30
Austin	8:15	9:15	4	$12	$22
San Francisco	8:30	9:50	3	$16	$28
White Plains	8:35	10:05	2	$22	$40
Chicago	8:45	11:45	1	$35	$65

Does the train to Seattle leave at nine o'clock?

No, it doesn't. It leaves at eight o'clock.

1. Does the train to Austin leave from track five?

2. Does the trip to San Francisco take one hour ten minutes?

3. Does the trip to White Plains cost twenty dollars one way?

4. Does the trip to Chicago cost seventy-five dollars round trip?

C. Answer the questions.

When does the train arrive in Seattle?

It arrives at nine fifteen.

1. When does the train arrive in Austin?

2. When does the train to San Francisco leave?

3. Which track does the train to White Plains leave from?

4. How much does a one-way ticket to Chicago cost?

5. How much does a round-trip ticket to Seattle cost?

6. How long does the trip to Austin take?

_____

7. How long does the trip to Chicago take?

_____

8. Which track does the train to Austin leave from?

_____

9. When does the train arrive in Chicago?

_____

10. When does the train arrive in White Plains?

_____

11. How much does a round-trip ticket to Austin cost?

_____

12. How long does the trip to Seattle take?

_____

D. Make a conversation.

What can I do for you?

When _____

It leaves at _____

Which _____

It leaves from _____

How long _____

The trip takes _____

When _____

It arrives at _____

How much _____

A one-way costs _____

How much _____

A round-trip costs _____

_____ , please.

That's _____

CONVERSATION

A. Complete the conversation.

Waiter! Excuse me!

_____

Please bring _____

   Another _____?

Yes, I don't have one.

_____

Thank you.

   Anything _____?

Yes, _____

   Don't you have one?

Yes, but my guest _____

_____

Thank you, and please _____

_____

   Right away. Do you need anything else?

_____

Right away.

B. Make a conversation.

You and your guest are in a restaurant.   You do not have a saucer.
The waiter is very bad.   You have a dirty plate.
You do not have a knife or a spoon.   Your guest has a dirty napkin.
Your guest does not have a fork or a cup.   You have no menu.

You: _____

Waiter: _____

You: _____

Waiter: _____

You: _____

Waiter: _____

You: _____

Waiter: _____

You: _____

Waiter: _____

You: _____

Waiter: _____

You: _____

Waiter: _____

A. Read the story.

Jake's Place is not the best place in town. It is not popular at all. Jake is the chef but he does not know how to cook. The coffee is always cold. The juice is always warm. The pizzas are overdone and the hamburgers are underdone.

His son, Jake Junior, is the waiter but he does not know how to wait on tables. The tables are always dirty.

His father, Jake Senior, is the cashier, but he does not know how to count. He always gives the wrong change.

His grandfather, Big Jake, is the dishwasher, but he is extremely clumsy. Most of the cups, glasses and plates are cracked or broken.

Jenny, his wife, runs the delivery service. She does not know how to drive. She delivers pizzas on her bike. This takes a long time, so the pizzas are usually very cold by the time she arrives.

B. Answer the questions.

1. What does Jake do for a living?

   _____

2. Why are the pizzas overdone?

   _____

3. What does Jake Junior do?

   _____

4. Why are the tables always dirty?

   _____

5. Why are the glasses cracked or broken?

   _____

6. Why do people get the wrong change?

   _____

7. Why are the pizzas cold by the time Jenny arrives?

   _____

8. Why does Jenny ride a bike?

   _____

9. Why do people go to Jake's Place?

   _____

A. Read the story.

Harry works as a cashier at a gas station. He goes to night school once a week. He takes an auto engineering course because he wants to become a mechanic. The class starts at seven and ends at nine each Monday evening. The course runs for ninety hours. Harry goes to school for ten weeks in the fall, ten weeks in the winter, and ten weeks in the spring. There are no evening classes in the summer.

B. Answer the questions.

1. Is Harry an attendant or a cashier?

   _____

2. Why does he take evening classes?

   _____

3. What day does he go to school?

   _____

4. Does he go to school in the morning and afternoon?

   _____

5. How many hours does the course run?

   _____

6. How many weeks does Harry go to school in the winter?

   _____

7. What time does each class start?

   _____

8. When does each class end?

   _____

9. Why doesn't Harry go to school in the summer?

   _____

A. Read the story.

Ria lives about thirty-five miles from town. She takes the bus to work every morning. She is a nurse and works at a hospital for the elderly.

She gets up at four thirty every morning although she does not start work until nine. Her bus leaves at a quarter to eight and the trip takes about an hour. It takes about five minutes for her to walk from the bus station to the hospital.

But why does Ria get up so early?

Well, she owns a small farm. She keeps two dozen hens and sells the eggs to the hospital. She breeds dogs and sells the puppies to the pet store. She raises turkeys and sells them to the supermarket at Thanksgiving.

And, of course, when she gets home each evening, she milks her cow!

B. Answer the questions.

1. Where does Ria live?

_____

2. Does she live in an apartment?

_____

3. How does she get to work each day?

_____

4. When does she get up?

_____

5. Why does she get up so early?

_____

6. Why does she keep hens?

_____

7. Why does she breed dogs?

_____

8. Why does she raise turkeys?

_____

9. What does she do when she gets home each evening?

_____

READING COMPREHENSION

A. Read the story.

Old Charlie

One day, after more than seventy years as a waiter, Old Charlie dies. Gloria, his best friend and customer for most of those years, is, of course, very sad. She is so sad she never sits at her old table any longer.

The new waiter is not half as good as Old Charlie. He is clumsy. He drops plates and cups. He is forgetful. He does not remember knives and forks and spoons. He is slow. The coffee is always cold when it arrives.

One evening after a hard day at the factory, Gloria comes into the restaurant and sits down at a table. Suddenly, she hears her name and sees a figure in the corner of the room.

"Gloria. It's me."

She cannot believe her ears.

"Charlie? Charlie! Is that you?" she asks.

"Yes, it's me," answers the figure.

"Come over here," says Gloria.

"I can't," answers the old waiter. "That's not my table!"

B. Answer the questions.

1. What was Old Charlie's job?

_____

2. Why is Gloria unhappy?

_____

3. Why does the new waiter drop things?

_____

4. Why is the coffee always cold?

_____

5. Why does Gloria sit at a different table?

_____

6. Why can't Old Charlie wait on her table?

_____

84

REVIEW
VOCABULARY

A. What's the job?

1. She rings up checks and makes change. _____

2. He takes orders at the restaurant. _____

3. She cooks food. _____

4. She waits on tables. _____

5. He fills your car with gas. _____

6. He gives you money at the bank. _____

7. She can fix your car. _____

8. She sews clothes. _____

CONVERSATION

B. Choose the correct alternatives.

1. Something to drink?
   a) Chicken breast, please.
   b) One slice, please.
   c) No, thank you.
2. I need some salt.
   a) They're over there.
   b) It's on the counter.
   c) Small, medium or large?

3. How long does it take?
   a) It's five kilometers.
   b) Ten minutes.
   c) It's five minutes slow.
4. Anything else?
   a) Oh, sorry.
   b) Right away.
   c) No, thanks.

QUESTIONS

A. Make questions to these answers.

1. _____

   It leaves at five o'clock.

2. _____

   It arrives at eight o'clock.

3. _____

   It takes one and a half hours.

4. _____

   A round trip costs forty dollars.

VOCABULARY BUILDING

B. Choose the correct alternative. There are new words here so try your best!

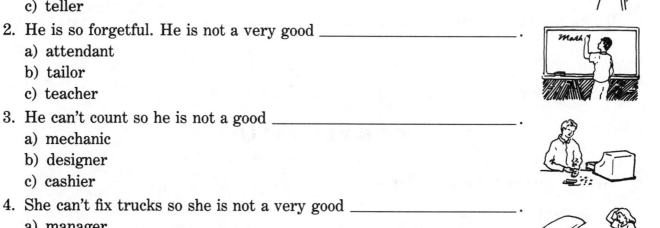

1. She is so clumsy. She is not a very good _____.
   a) waitress
   b) tenant
   c) teller

2. He is so forgetful. He is not a very good _____.
   a) attendant
   b) tailor
   c) teacher

3. He can't count so he is not a good _____.
   a) mechanic
   b) designer
   c) cashier

4. She can't fix trucks so she is not a very good _____.
   a) manager
   b) doctor
   c) mechanic

5. He can't draw so he is not a very good _____.
   a) nurse
   b) doctor
   c) architect

CONVERSATION

A. Make a conversation.

You and your friend are at the restaurant.
You call the waitress because you don't have a napkin.
The waitress asks if you need anything else.
You ask for another cup of coffee for your friend because the coffee is cold.
The waitress is very sorry of course.

You: _____

Waitress: _____

You: _____

Waitress: _____

You: _____

Waitress: _____

BAY CITY NEWS CROSSWORD

B. Fill in the crossword puzzle. Use textbook pages 85–87 for help.

DOWN

1. The small trees are on _____ .
2. The parade was a big _____ .
4. The money you get for your work every month.
5. Blue is my _____ color.
6. They sell flowers and _____ .
8. The money children get from their parents.
10. Not unfurnished.
11. 250 watts of _____ .
12. She works _____ time at the factory.
13. They are a one _____ family, just father and daughter.
14. It's cold. You'll need your _____ .
15. Not morning.

ACROSS

3. The Mall looks _____ .
5. After Thursday.
7. Litter.
9. A "book" with all the months.
14. Winter is my favorite _____ .
16. On _____ it needs 250 watts of power.
17. I was bad when I was a _____ .
18. _____ is good. We sell a lot.
19. I need a person with _____ .
20. The apartment has pool _____ .

A. Look at the picture of the hospital. Discuss the hospital.

B. Read the crossword clues.

DOWN

1. Between the fourth and the sixth.
3. The florist is to the _____ of the reception desk.
4. After the second.
5. The _____ shop is next to the florist.
6. The babies are in the _____ .
7. The _____ is in the basement.
10. Ask the _____ where the cafeteria is.
11. Read the third _____ from the top.
12. The reception desk is on the first _____ .
13. The doctor is in the _____ room.
15. The _____ shop is to the right of the reception desk.
16. The _____ therapy unit is on the second floor.
19. The _____ unit is on the third floor.
20. Take the _____ or the elevator.
22. The physical therapy unit is on the _____ floor.
23. _____ your left eye and read the first line.
25. Cover your right eye and read the _____ .

ACROSS

2. Before the second.
8. Let's have coffee in the _____ .
9. The _____ is helping the patient.
11. The cafeteria is to the _____ of the x-ray unit.
14. The computer _____ is on the third floor.
16. The _____ is next to the cafeteria.
17. The doctor is in the emergency _____ .
18. The nurse is helping the _____ .
21. Take the stairs or the _____ to the third floor.
24. The physical _____ unit is on the second floor.
26. Cover one _____ and read the chart.
27. The chapel is in the _____ .
28. Please _____ the fifth line from the top.

C. Use the picture and the clues. Fill in the crossword puzzle.

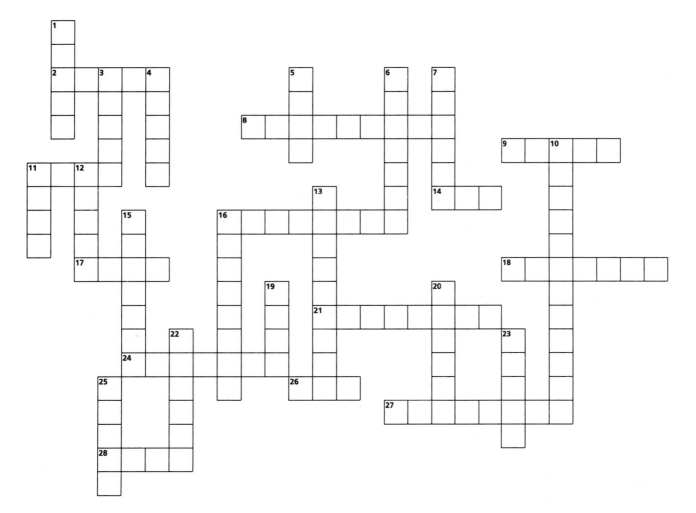

D. Answer the questions.

1. Where is the gift shop?

   _____

2. Where are the babies?

   _____

3. Where is the chapel?

   _____

4. What is the nurse doing?

   _____

5. Where is the cafeteria?

   _____

6. Which floor is the reception desk on?

   _____

7. Where is the doctor?

   _____

8. Where is the x-ray unit?

   _____

A. Answer the questions.

1. When do you get up on workdays?

   _____

2. When do you leave your home?

   _____

3. How do you get to work?

   _____

4. How long do you work each day?

   _____

5. Where do you work?

   _____

6. When do you get home?

   _____

7. What do you like to do in your free time?

   _____

8. Do you have a family?

   _____

B. Ask a friend the same questions.

C. Write about your friend.

He/She gets up at _____

He/She leaves _____

_____

_____

_____

_____

_____

A. Read the story.

Doris loves her work. She gets up at four, has a quick cup of coffee and leaves her home at ten to five every morning, Monday to Friday. She takes the bus to town and arrives at work at about a quarter to six.

Doris cleans the offices before the other workers arrive at nine. She is very proud of her work. She is a very tidy person. Unfortunately, the others are not. They don't empty their waste paper baskets or their ashtrays. They don't pick up things from the floor. They don't change the filter in the coffee machine and they never, never wash their coffee cups.

Doris doesn't mind. The others don't keep the office tidy, so her job becomes more important. She always brews a pot of fresh coffee just before nine so that the others can start the day with fresh cups!

Answer the questions.

1. When does Doris get up?

_____

2. What does she do before she leaves home?

_____

3. How does she get to work?

_____

4. When does she arrive at work?

_____

5. What sort of person is she?

_____

C. Answer the questions. Follow the example.

Why does she empty the waste paper baskets?
Because the others don't empty the waste paper baskets.

1. Why does she empty the ashtrays?

_____

2. Why does she pick up things from the floor?

_____

3. Why does she change the filter in the coffee machine?

_____

4. Why does she wash the coffee cups?

_____

5. Why does she brew coffee just before nine?

_____

CONVERSATION

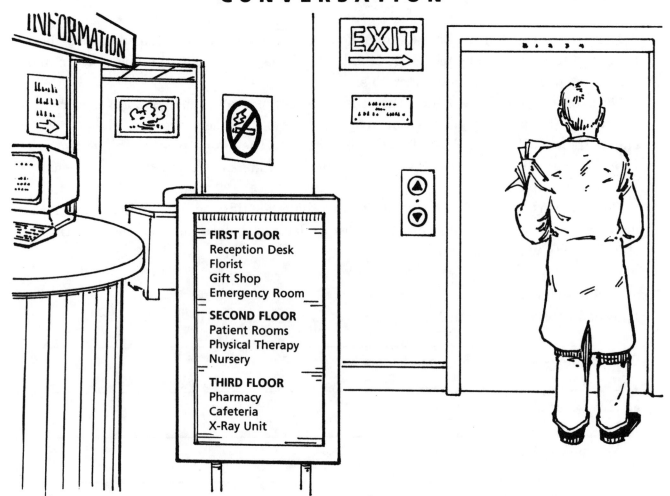

A. Look at the picture and complete the conversation.

1. Where's the Nursery, please?

   _____

2. Where's the Gift Shop?

   _____

3. Where is the Cafeteria?

   _____

B. Choose the correct alternatives.

1. My pleasure.
   a) Don't mention it.
   b) Yes, it is.
   c) No, it isn't.

2. Is X-ray in the basement?
   a) Yes, downstairs.
   b) Yes, up a flight.
   c) Yes, don't mention it.

3. Thank you.
   a) Take the escalator.
   b) My pleasure.
   c) Follow the broken line.

4. Is the florist on the first floor?
   a) Yes, it's in the basement.
   b) Yes, thank you.
   c) Yes, it's next to the Gift Shop.

VOCABULARY BUILDING

A. Look at the picture.

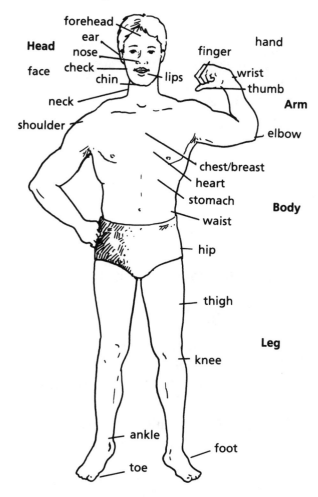

Head — forehead, ear, nose, check, chin, face, neck, shoulder, lips

Arm — finger, hand, wrist, thumb, elbow

Body — chest/breast, heart, stomach, waist, hip, thigh

Leg — knee, ankle, foot, toe

B. Read this.

He has a rash on his nose.

She has a sore on her knee.

They have cuts on their arms and legs.

I have a bandage on my finger.

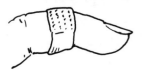

C. Describe the following.

1. _____

2. _____

3. _____

4. _____

A. Read the story.

My son has a serious problem. He is allergic to all sorts of food. My wife and two daughters don't have the same problems. For breakfast, we have corn flakes and milk and a cup of tea. Mark has a glass of water and corn flakes without milk.

For lunch, we sometimes have hamburgers and french fries. He has a tomato and a baked potato because he is allergic to dairy products like milk, cream, butter, and margarine.

If Mark has ice cream he immediately has a very high fever, so we never have ice cream in the house.

Mark also has a problem with most fruits. If he eats an orange or a grapefruit, for example, he has a terrible rash on his face, hands and body. If he eats cherries he has sores in his mouth for several days.

We all love animals, but we don't have a pet because Mark is allergic to them.

Answer the questions.

1. What problem does Mark have?

   _____

2. How many children does the man have?

   _____

3. What do the girls have for breakfast?

   _____

4. What does Mark have for breakfast?

   _____

5. Why doesn't Mark have ice cream?

   _____

6. Why doesn't he have cherries?

   _____

7. Why doesn't he have oranges?

   _____

8. Why don't they have a dog?

   _____

VOCABULARY BUILDING

A. Look at these essential pairs.

1. knife and fork

3. bike and pump

5. tennis racket & ball

2. cup and saucer

4. bacon and eggs

6. car & license

B. Fill in the missing words.

1. If you don't have a license, you don't need a _____ .
2. If you don't have a racket, the _____ are no good.
3. If you don't have a cup, you don't need a _____ .
4. If you get a flat and you don't have a _____ , you can't ride your _____ .
5. If you don't have a _____ and fork you can't eat your _____ and _____ .

C. Describe these people.

_____He has a knife, but he doesn't have a fork._____
_____

_____They have bacon, but they don't have eggs._____
_____

1. _____
_____

2. _____
_____

3. _____
_____

4. _____
_____

95

READING COMPREHENSION

A. Read the story.

Sam's Doctor Visit

Sam feels sick so he goes to see his friend the doctor. The doctor is, as usual, very sympathetic.

What can I do for you, Sam?

I'm ill, really ill, Doc.

What are the symptoms, Sam?

I have a rash on my stomach, chest and back. And I feel sick.

Oh, dear.

And I have sores in my mouth and on my lips.

How amazing! And do you see spots in front of your eyes?

Yes, Doc. That's right! How clever of you!

And do you have a headache and a sore throat?

Absolutely!

And do you feel sick in the morning before breakfast?

Exactly so!

And do you have a slight cold?

Yes, just a slight cold, nothing big.

And you have a backache, of course.

Fantastic. That's exactly right.

And do you feel tired after lunch and do you sleep all afternoon?

You describe my symptoms perfectly! What's wrong with me?

I don't know, but I have exactly the same symptoms. I wonder what it is!

B. Answer the questions.

1. Where do Sam and the doctor have a rash?

_____

2. Where do they have sores?

_____

3. How do they feel before breakfast?

_____

4. Where do they feel sore?

_____

5. How do they feel after lunch?

_____

6. What do they do all afternoon?

_____

7. What does the doctor describe?

_____

8. What doesn't the doctor know?

_____

REVIEW
VOCABULARY

A. Use the pictures to complete the sentences.

1. On my way home I stop at the _____
   to pick up my clothes.

2. On his way home he stops at the _____
   to buy medicine.

3. On her way home she stops at the _____
   to fill up the car.

4. On their way home they stop at the _____
   to get some money.

5. On our way home we stop at the _____
   to buy some flowers.

CONVERSATION

B. Look at the eye chart and answer True or False.

A	Y	F	E	I	K
L	Q	B	X	N	S
J	G	R	P	O	U
D	W	T	H	Z	C

1. A is the first letter on the first line. [T] [ ]
2. B is the second letter from the right. [ ] [ ]
3. C is the last letter on the fourth line. [ ] [ ]
4. I is the second letter from the left
   on the first line. [ ] [ ]
5. P is the third letter on the fourth line. [ ] [ ]

C. Look at the eye chart again. Where are these?

1. X is _____

2. R is _____

3. H is _____

4. Z is _____

5. K is _____

VOCABULARY BUILDING

A. Choose the best alternatives. There are new words here so try your best!

1. Take the escalator to the _____ .
   a) yard
   b) second floor
   c) elevator

   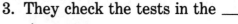

2. Let's have a drink in the _____ .
   a) chapel
   b) stairs
   c) cafeteria

3. They check the tests in the _____ .
   a) nursery
   b) lab
   c) florist

4. The heart attack patient is in the _____ .
   a) emergency room
   b) pharmacy
   c) opticians

B. Make questions for the answers.

1. _____

   I leave home at about seven-thirty.

2. _____

   She arrives at work at about nine.

3. _____

   I sometimes stop at the library.

4. _____

   He goes home at six.

5. _____

   We take the bus to work.

6. _____

   They drink coffee.

C. Answer the questions.

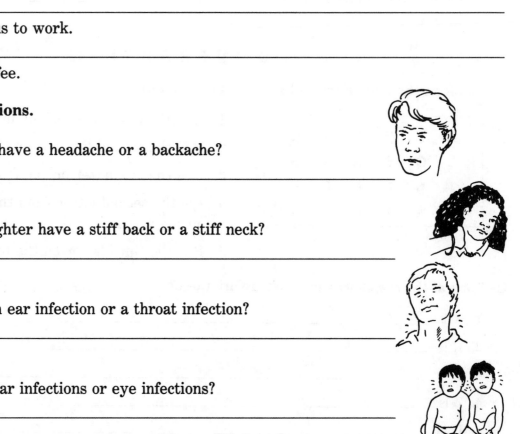

1. Does your son have a headache or a backache?

   _____

2. Does your daughter have a stiff back or a stiff neck?

   _____

3. Do you have an ear infection or a throat infection?

   _____

4. Do they have ear infections or eye infections?

   _____

BAY CITY NEWS CROSSWORD

Fill in the crossword puzzle. Use textbook pages 97–99 for help.

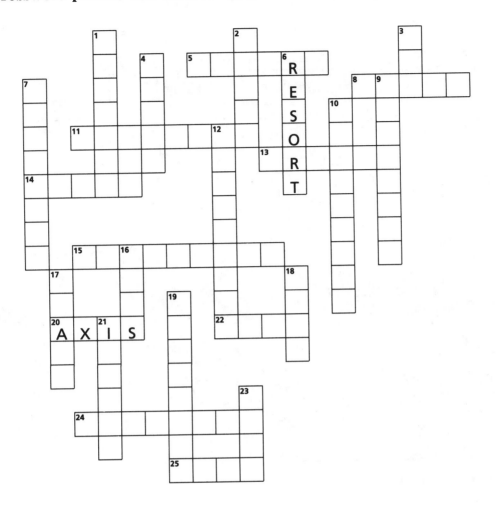

DOWN

1. Some people wake up _____ an alarm.
2. They forecast only _____ snow.
3. Local time is the time by the _____ .
4. For sale by _____ .
6. I go to a ski _____ in winter.
7. I am a _____ of this apartment.
9. The children play _____ .
10. She works at home. She is a _____ .
12. There was a heavy _____ .
16. _____ than two inches of snow.
17. Some people wake up with an _____ .
18. Not difficult.
19. I work _____ on Sundays.
21. Two _____ of snow.
23. Not east.

ACROSS

5. The _____ love the snow.
8. There are different time _____ .
11. The _____ is for light snow.
13. The apartment is on the _____ floor.
14. Jean survived after his _____ .
15. I am _____ to hear that.
20. The earth rotates on its _____ .
22. The roads were a _____ !
24. Linda Prose said the snowstorm was _____ .
25. Not west.

A. Look at the picture of the traffic jam. Discuss the traffic jam.

CAR POOL LANE

STOP KING ST.

SUBWAY

BUS STOP

B. Read the crossword clues.

DOWN

1. The _____ entrance is next to the bus stop.
2. The traffic _____ stops the traffic.
3. A _____ is on the sidwalk.
5. I go _____ bus to work each day.
6. Take the _____ to the island.
8. Take the _____ to New York.
9. _____ trains in Cleveland.
10. Busses, cars and trucks are _____ .
11. Take the _____ car up the hill.
14. The _____ is in front of the tow truck.
16. There is a _____ at the traffic light.
17. The _____ jam is very bad.
18. The car _____ lane is empty.
19. One way or _____ trip?
23. The car pool _____ is empty.
26. The bus _____ is next to the subway entrance.

ACROSS

4. The children go by _____ to school.
7. A _____ is next to the car on the sidewalk.
12. A one _____ ticket to Cleveland, please.
13. The _____ is behind the bus.
15. Take a _____ . It's faster.
17. One way or round _____ ?
20. _____ way, please.
21. We _____ to work in the city each day.
22. An _____ is behind the trolley.
24. A car and a motorcycle are on the _____ .
25. A _____ is sitting on the sidewalk.
27. The tow _____ is pulling the bus.
28. The _____ is on King Street.
29. The telephone _____ is across the street.
30. The car crashed into the traffic _____ .

C. Use the picture and the clues. Fill in the crossword puzzle.

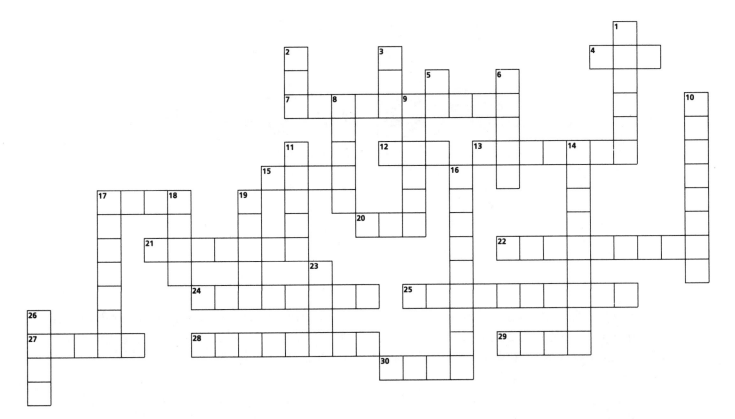

D. Answer the questions.

1. Where is the bus stop?

_____

2. How do the children get to school?

_____

3. What is on the sidewalk?

_____

4. How do you get to the island?

_____

5. What is next to the car on the sidewalk?

_____

6. How do you get up the hill?

_____

7. What is the tow truck doing?

_____

8. Where is the limousine?

_____

A. Read the story.

Sandra Manlem says she enjoys her work. She runs a small company, Fast Efficient Fish, that buys fish from fishermen at the harbor and sells it to hotels along the beach. She employs five people and pays them by the hour because she never knows how much work she has for the day.

Some days, the fishermen return late because of bad weather or because the fishing was not good. This annoys her because it delays her workers. Many of the small hotels rely on Sandra for their fish but she must deliver it in time for lunch.

If she is late too often, it destroys her reputation for Fast Efficient Fish.

Answer the questions.

1. Why are the fishermen late sometimes?

_____

2. How many people does Sandra employ?

_____

3. How does she pay them?

_____

4. Why does she pay them by the hour?

_____

5. What does her company buy?

_____

6. Who does she sell the fish to?

_____

7. Why must she deliver the fish in time?

_____

8. Why does she not want to be late too often?

_____

A. Read the story.

Mark worries a lot about his hair. He always carries a brush and comb in his pocket wherever he goes. As soon as he enters a building he hurries to the bathroom to check his hair. He tries to look his best at all times. Of course, if you ask him why he worries so much about his hair, he denies it.

"My hair? What about my hair? I never worry about my hair," he replies.

But we all know it is not true. Poor old Mark worries about his hair all the time. If he cannot find a mirror in a bathroom he relies on his reflection in shop windows.

The other day, Mark was in front of me in the bus. He is a bit thin on top. Now I understand why he worries so much!

B. Answer the questions.

1. What does Mark worry about?

_____

2. What does he always carry in his pocket?

_____

3. What does he do as soon as he gets indoors?

_____

4. Why does he go to the bathroom?

_____

5. What does Mark always try to do?

_____

6. What does he do if you ask him why he worries?

_____

7. If there is no mirror, what does he rely on?

_____

8. Why does Mark worry so much?

_____

C. Answer the questions your own way.

1. What do you worry about?

_____

2. What does your best friend worry about?

_____

3. What do you always try to do?

_____

4. What does your best friend always try to do?

_____

CONVERSATION

A. Complete the conversation.

Is that job still open?

_____

I think so.
   Good. What's your name?

_____

   Can you spell that?

_____

   Are you employed at the moment?

Yes, _____
   How long have you worked there?

_____

   Do you have any experience for this job?

Yes, _____

B. Choose the correct alternatives.

1. I'm out of work.
   a) How long have you been unemployed?
   b) That's a long time.
   c) Experience is required.
2. How long have you worked there?
   a) About a month.
   b) I'm not happy there.
   c) I'm out of work.

3. That's a long time.
   a) I'm out of work.
   b) Spell that, please.
   c) There are no jobs around.

4. I have no experience.
   a) I work at a bank.
   b) Sorry, experience required.
   c) Practice with your partner.

C. Make a conversation.

You interview for a job as a mechanic.
You have some experience.
You work at Josie's Gas Station.
You have worked there for 1 year.
You are not happy there because the pay is not good.

You: _____

Boss: _____

You: _____

Boss: _____

You: _____

Boss: _____

You: _____

VOCABULARY BUILDING

A. Read this.

Tim

He washes his hair with shampoo and conditioner. He dries his hair. Then he brushes and combs it.

Tina

She washes her clothes in the washing machine. She dries them in the dryer or hangs them on the line. Then she irons them.

Tony

He changes the blade in his razor. He puts shaving cream on his face with a brush. Then he has a nice clean shave. Sometimes he uses an electric razor. It is not as good, but it is faster!

Tania

First she uses an eyeliner on her eyelids. Then she adds a little mascara to her eyelashes. Then she puts blush on her cheeks and lipstick on her lips. Finally, she adds a spot of perfume on her neck.

B. Answer the questions.

1. How does Tim wash his hair?

_____

2. What does he do after he dries it?

_____

3. How does Tina dry her clothes?

_____

4. What does she do after she dries them?

_____

5. How does Tony put cream on his face?

_____

6. Why does he sometimes use an electric razor?

_____

7. Where does Tania use mascara?

_____

8. Where does she put her perfume?

_____

Answer the questions.

1. What does he polish?

_____

2. What do they polish?

_____

3. What does she catch?

_____

4. Who does he kiss?

_____

5. What do they watch?

_____

6. Where do they hurry to?

_____

7. What does he worry about?

_____

8. How many men does he employ?

_____

9. What do they carry?

_____

VOCABULARY BUILDING

A. Read the story about Sam.

Sam is very interested in home decorating. He always wallpapers one room each season. He repapers the living room in the spring, and the bedroom in the summer. He repapers the bathroom in the fall and the kitchen in the winter. First he strips off the old paper. Then he paints around the windows and along the floor and ceiling. Sometimes he even paints the ceiling and the floor before he does the windows. Finally he hangs the new wallpaper. His house is always fresh and clean because smoking is not allowed!

B. Answer the questions.

1. What does Sam do each season?

_____

2. What does he do before he paints around the windows?

_____

3. What does he sometimes do before he paints around the windows?

_____

4. What does he do after he paints around the windows?

_____

5. Why is his house always fresh and clean?

_____

C. Read the story about Sandra.

Sandra is very interested in cars. She always fixes her car if it breaks down. She changes her tire if she has a flat. First she applies the hand brake. Then she loosens the wheel nuts before she jacks up the car. She removes the old tire and puts on the spare. Then she tightens the bolts and releases the jack.

D. Answer the questions.

1. What does Sandra do if her car breaks down?

_____

2. What does she do if she has a flat?

_____

3. What does she do before she loosens the wheel nuts?

_____

4. What does she do after she removes the old tire?

_____

5. What does she do after she puts on the spare tire?

_____

READING COMPREHENSION

A. Read the story.

The Talking Dog

Mary goes into a restaurant one afternoon. She has her dog with her. She sits down at a table near the window. Her dog sits on the chair across from her. The waiter comes over to take her order.

"I am sorry. Dogs are not allowed in the restaurant."

"But my dog is very special. He is a talking dog."

"That makes no difference. The dog is not allowed."

But Mary refuses to leave. So the waiter calls the manager.

"I am sorry. Dogs are not allowed in the restaurant."

"But my dog is very special. He is a talking dog."

"If he is a talking dog, let me hear him talk!"

"All right. Ask him a question."

The manager looks at the dog. The dog looks at the manager.

"What is above this restaurant?"

"R-r-r-oof! R-r-r-oof!"

"That dog cannot talk! It can only bark! Out! Both of you!"

Mary and her dog leave the restaurant. Outside, the dog looks up at the roof and then looks at Mary and says, "Sorry, Mary. There is a hairdressing salon above the restaurant! I didn't know."

B. Answer the questions.

1. Where does Mary sit?

_____

2. Where does the dog sit?

_____

3. Why must the dog leave?

_____

4. Why does the manager come over?

_____

5. Why does the dog give the wrong answer?

_____

REVIEW

Answer the questions.

1. Does he fry one egg or two eggs?

_____

2. Does she carry a table or a chair?

_____

3. Do they pay five dollars or ten dollars?

_____

4. Do you like apples or oranges?

_____

5. Do we begin at eight or at nine?

_____

6. Does he employ three men or four men?

_____

7. Does she worry about her cat or her dog?

_____

8. Do they destroy the train or the plane?

_____

9. Does she enjoy tennis or golf?

_____

10. Do you enjoy football or baseball?

_____

11. Does he wash his hands or his face?

_____

12. Do they miss the bus or the train?

_____

13. Does he catch a fish or a bird?

_____

14. Does she kiss her husband or her baby?

_____

15. Do you leave home at six or at seven?

_____

Answer the questions your own way.

1. Are you tall, short or of medium height?

   _____

2. Are you slim, chubby or of medium build?

   _____

3. Is your best friend tall or short?

   _____

4. Is your neighbor chubby or slim?

   _____

5. Are the children good or bad?

   _____

6. Are you two interested in cars or home decoration?

   _____

7. Are your parents old or young?

   _____

8. Was the weather good or bad yesterday?

   _____

9. Was it sunny or rainy the day before yesterday?

   _____

10. How many students are there in your class?

    _____

11. Were there two people on the bus or was there only one?

    _____

12. What will the weather be like tomorrow?

    _____

13. What will the weather be like the day after tomorrow?

    _____

14. What time is it now?

    _____

15. How many rooms are there in your home?

    _____

BAY CITY NEWS CROSSWORD

Fill in the crossword puzzle. Use textbook pages 109–111 for help.

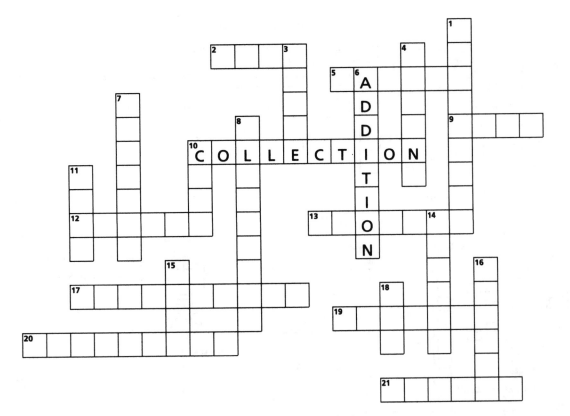

DOWN

1. 20% _____ for the elderly.
3. The flamingos are to _____ money.
4. Your world for a _____ .
6. It's the latest _____ to the collection.
7. The _____ is of a flower.
8. Hire pink _____ for a day.
10. A big town.
11. The same as "hire."
14. You must _____ the flamingo by 5 p.m.
15. We are _____ every day.
16. Mahogany and teak are _____ .
18. A parking _____ .

ACROSS

2. They pay by the _____ .
5. She is a _____ artist.
9. Palm and patchouli are _____ .
10. A _____ of famous drawings.
12. 90.
13. A drawing of _____ .
17. No _____ to the rules!
19. A stop smoking _____ .
20. Quinine and aspirin are _____ .
21. Jute and rattan are _____ .

A. Look at the picture of the airport. Discuss the airport.

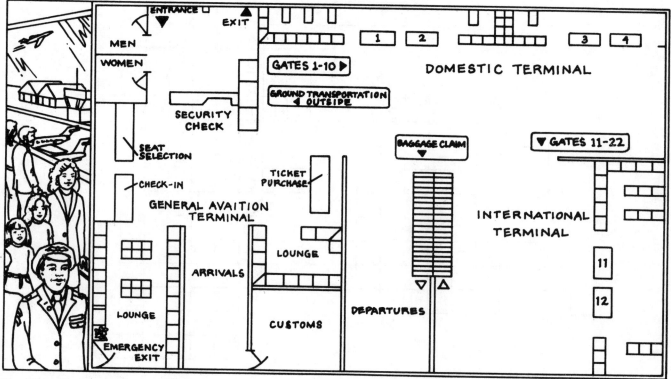

B. Read the crossword clues.

DOWN

1. Are you on business or _____ ?
3. Please pass through the _____ check.
4. Only passengers with tickets can pass through the security _____ .
6. Is this the _____ Terminal or the Domestic Terminal?
7. I'm hungry. I need a _____ .
10. Check your _____ at the Check-in Desk.
11. Don't park your car in front of the _____ exit.
14. The Baggage _____ is in the basement.
16. Do you have a _____ pass?
17. Please show me your _____ .
18. Is this the _____ Terminal?
20. The _____ Hall is to the left of the Departures Hall.
21. Which _____ do we leave from?
24. If you have no ticket, stand in line at the Ticket _____ Desk.
28. The _____ is next to the Check-in Desk.
30. I have _____ 35F.

ACROSS

1. Do you have a boarding _____ ?
2. I'm going to China on _____ .
4. I'm traveling first _____ to Egypt.
5. I'll wait for you outside the _____ .
8. Where are the gates? Just follow the _____ .
9. This is the International _____ .
12. Let's have a drink in the _____ .
13. Where can I _____ my luggage?
15. The _____ Claim is in the basement.
19. Are we _____ class or coach?
22. Ground _____ to the other terminal is outside.
23. The _____ are next to the Security Check.
25. The General _____ Terminal is next to the Domestic Terminal.
26. The _____ are in the Arrivals Hall.
27. The Seat _____ Desk is next to the Check-in Desk.
29. Let's take a _____ from the airport to downtown.
31. This is the wrong way. Let's go _____ the way we came.
32. The _____ Aviation Terminal is over there.
33. The _____ Hall is next to the Arrivals Hall.

C. Use the pictures and the clues. Fill in the crossword puzzle.

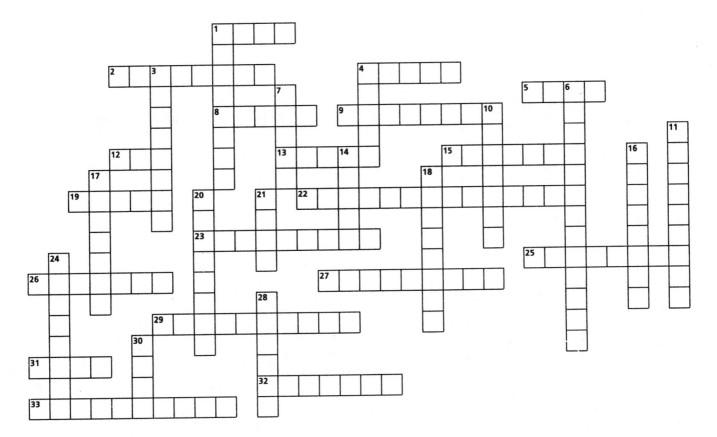

D. Answer the questions.

1. Where is the emergency exit?

_____

2. Where is the International Terminal?

_____

3. Where are the men's restrooms?

_____

4. Where is the Ground Transportation?

_____

5. Where is the Security Check?

_____

6. Where is the Lounge?

_____

7. Where is Gate 21?

_____

8. What gates are for domestic departure?

_____

A. Answer the questions.

1. Is Tim taller than Rick?

   _____

2. Is Rick taller than Tom?

   _____

3. Is Tom taller than Tim?

   _____

4. Who is the tallest?

   _____

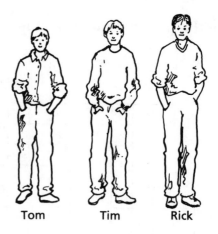

Tom   Tim   Rick

B. Answer the questions.

1. Is Colby as fat as Sammy?

   _____

2. Is Sammy as fat as Wally?

   _____

3. Is Wally as fat as Colby?

   _____

4. Which is the fattest puppy?

   _____

Colby   Sammy   Wally

C. Answer the questions.

1. Is Puff chubbier than Blackie?

   _____

2. Is Blackie as chubby as Fuzzy?

   _____

3. Is Fuzzy as chubby as Puff?

   _____

4. Which is the chubbiest cat?

   _____

Puff   Blackie   Fuzzy

D. Answer the questions.

1. Does Gail have curlier hair than Janet?

   _____

2. Does Janet have curlier hair than Tammy?

   _____

3. Does Tammy have curlier hair than Gail?

   _____

4. Who has the curliest hair?

   _____

Gail   Janet   Tammy

A. Read this.

Athletes	Swimming 50 meters	High Jump	Long Jump	Sprint 100 m	Javelin
Clare	560	530	690	230	400
Lucy	570	430	500	400	200
Jenny	350	560	320	560	100

Clare, Lucy and Jenny are taking part in an athletic contest. Here are the points they have in each event. Clare has most points. She wins the gold medal. Lucy is the second best and wins the silver medal. Jenny is in third place and wins the bronze medal.

B. Answer the questions.

1. Is Clare better or worse than Lucy at swimming?

_____

2. Is Clare better or worse than Jenny at swimming?

_____

3. Is Lucy better or worse than Jenny at the high jump?

_____

4. Is Jenny better or worse than Clare at the long jump?

_____

5. Is Lucy better or worse than Jenny at the 100 meters?

_____

6. Is Jenny better or worse than Clare at the javelin?

_____

7. Who is the best swimmer?

_____

8. Who is the worst javelin thrower?

_____

9. Who is the best high jumper?

_____

10. Who is the worst long jumper?

_____

11. Who is the best sprinter?

_____

CONVERSATION

A. Make a conversation.

You are away from home.
You call home on Tuesday.
You will be home the day after tomorrow at five in the morning.
The weather is cold and windy but at home it is warm and dry.

_____

_____

_____

_____

_____

_____

_____

B. Complete the sentences.

1. It's cold outside so you'll need your _____ .
   a) bathing suit   b) overcoat   c) underwear
2. It's rainy outside so you'll need your _____ .
   a) umbrella   b) groceries   c) breakfast
3. It's windy outside so you'll need your _____ .
   a) cough medicine   b) sunglasses   c) scarf
4. It's mild outside so you'll need your _____ .
   a) sandals   b) overcoat   c) costume
5. It's freezing outside so you'll need your _____ .
   a) gloves   b) addition   c) pool

C. Complete the conversation.

Hello, it's me.

_____

I'm in Sweden.

_____

It's cold and damp.

_____

Next Sunday.

_____

I arrive at six in the afternoon.

_____

Okay, see you then!

VOCABULARY BUILDING

Look at the pictures. Then complete the sentences.

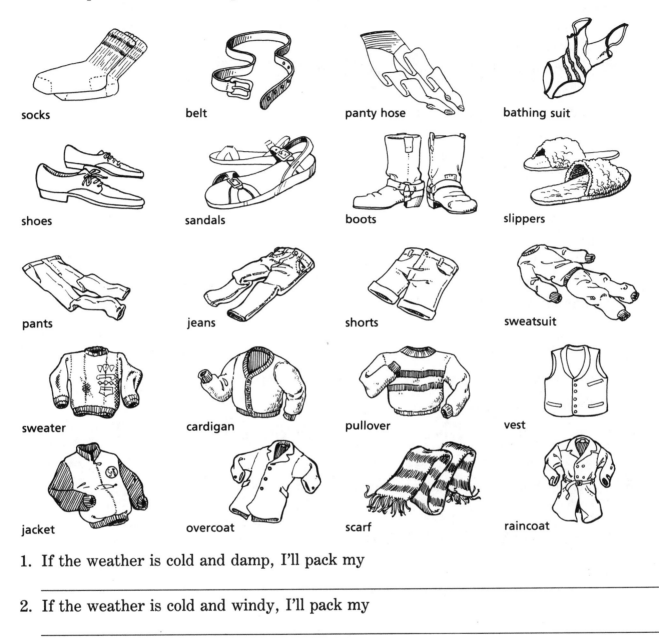

socks   belt   panty hose   bathing suit

shoes   sandals   boots   slippers

pants   jeans   shorts   sweatsuit

sweater   cardigan   pullover   vest

jacket   overcoat   scarf   raincoat

1. If the weather is cold and damp, I'll pack my
   _____

2. If the weather is cold and windy, I'll pack my
   _____

3. If the weather is mild and rainy, I'll pack my
   _____

4. If the weather is chilly and foggy, I'll pack my
   _____

5. If the weather is warm and sunny, I'll pack my
   _____

6. If the weather is hot and sticky, I'll pack my
   _____

7. If the weather is freezing and snowy, I'll pack my
   _____

A. Choose the correct alternatives.

1. Why are you going to the laundromat?
   a) I have to pick up my laundry.
   b) We have to return a book.
   c) She has to vacuum.
2. Why are you going to see your neighbor?
   a) I have to scrub the toilet.
   b) They have to take a poll.
   c) We have to baby-sit.
3. Why does he have to go out?
   a) He has to vacuum.
   b) He has to empty the trash.
   c) He has to scrub the floor.
4. Why do they have to go to town?
   a) They have to pick up some groceries.
   b) They have to dust the furniture.
   c) They have to wash the dishes.

B. Answer the questions.

1. What do you have to do if all your dishes are dirty?

   I have to wash the dishes.

2. What does he have to do if he wants to learn chemistry?

3. What does she have to do if all her clothes are dirty?

4. What do they have to do if their floor is very, very dirty?

5. Where do you two have to go if you want to borrow books?

6. What does grandmother have to do if mother and father want to go out?

7. What do you have to do if your hair is too long?

8. What does she have to do if the grass gets too long?

A. Fill in the chart.

Put the names of your family across the top of the chart. Mark with a cross (x) what each person does around the house.
Note: If you do not have a family, think of a friend or neighbor.

Chores						
washing dishes						
washing windows						
cleaning bathroom						
scrubbing floor						
vacuuming						
dusting						
ironing						
doing laundry						
emptying garbage						
mowing lawn						
washing car						
cooking						
grocery shopping						

B. Answer the questions your own way.

Describe all the household chores you, or the family members have to do. Use some of the following words: every day, every Saturday, every week, every two weeks, every month, every year, every two years.

1. Every day, I have to _____
2. _____
3. _____
4. _____
5. _____
6. _____
7. _____
8. _____

READING COMPREHENSION

A. Read the story.

My New Job

I am going to start my new job on Monday. And the most wonderful thing about my job is that every day is a holiday.

How can every day be a holiday? The answer is simple.

There are three hundred and sixty-five days in a year, or three hundred and sixty-six days if it is a Leap Year.

If a working day is eight hours long, that is a third of a day, because a day has twenty-four hours.

A third of three hundred and sixty-six is one hundred and twenty-two. So I work one hundred and twenty-two days a year.

Now, nobody works on Sundays. There are fifty-two Sundays a year so there are only seventy working days left.

I have two weeks' vacation, fourteen days. This leaves only fifty-six days.

Of course, there is also Christmas Day, New Year's Eve, New Year's Day, and the Fourth of July. That leaves only fifty-two days.

Oh, by the way, nobody works on Saturdays. There are fifty-two Saturdays in a year so that is the end of my working days!

B. Answer the questions.

1. How many hours are there in a day?

   _____

2. How many days are there in a week?

   _____

3. How many weeks are there in a month?

   _____

4. How many months are there in a year?

   _____

5. What are the names of the seasons in a year?

   _____

6. How long is his vacation?

   _____

7. Which days does he not work on?

   _____

8. What is wrong with this calculation?

   _____

   _____

R E V I E W
V O C A B U L A R Y

A. Write to words for the pictures.

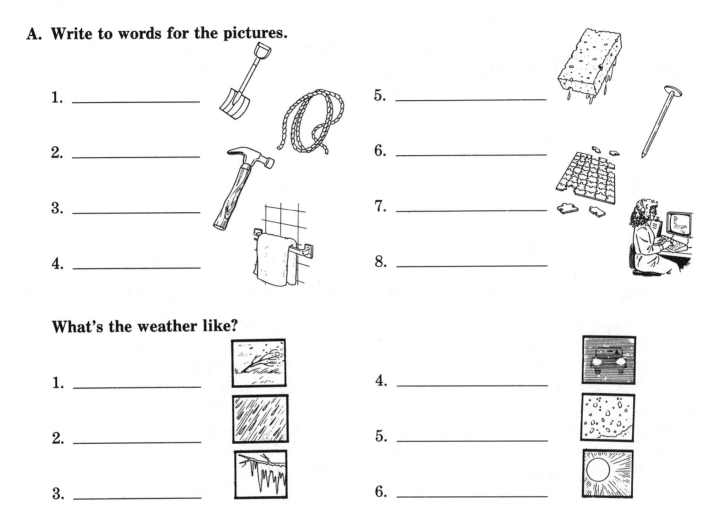

1. _____

2. _____

3. _____

4. _____

5. _____

6. _____

7. _____

8. _____

What's the weather like?

1. _____

2. _____

3. _____

4. _____

5. _____

6. _____

B. Fill in the missing words.

1. Is Mary as tall as Jack?

   No, Jack is _____ than Mary.

2. Is Jack as good as Mary at cooking?

   No, Mary is _____ than Jack.

3. Is Tom as bad as I am at golf?

   No, he is _____ than you at golf.

4. Is Peter as tall as you are?

   Oh, yes. He is _____ person I know.

5. Is Harry as good as you are at tennis?

   Oh, yes. He is _____ tennis player I know.

6. Is Jane as bad as I am at math?

   Oh, yes. She is _____ student in the class.

7. Is Janet as pretty as your sister?

   No, my sister is _____ Janet.

8. Is my dog as thin as your dog?

   No, my dog is _____ your dog.

9. Is this test as easy as the other one?

   Yes, this is _____ test in the book.

10. Is this box as big as the other one?

    Yes, this is _____ box I have.

11. Is his new movie as exciting as his first one?

    No, his first one was _____ than this one.

12. Was that dress as expensive as your old one?

    Yes, it was _____ dress in the shop.

VOCABULARY BUILDING

C. Choose the correct alternatives. There are new words here so try your best!

1. I'll be home on Thursday.
   a) It's cold—you'll need your sandals.
   b) Great. I miss you.
   c) What's the weather like?
2. What's it like at home?
   a) Not so good.
   b) Bye bye.
   c) I'll be home tomorrow.
3. Are you home already?
   a) Hi! It's me.
   b) I'll be staying a month.
   c) No, I'm still in Rome.
4. See you soon.
   a) Welcome home!
   b) Hurry home.
   c) Yes, I will.

CONVERSATION

D. Complete the conversation.

Hello. It's me.

_____

I'm still in Cairo.

_____

It's hot and sticky.

_____

I'll be home on Thursday.

_____

At six thirty in the evening.

_____

Great! I'll wait outside the terminal.

BAY CITY NEWS CROSSWORD

Fill in the crossword puzzle. Use textbook pages 121–123 for help.

DOWN

1. The same as shoreline.
2. Before February.
4. The Atlantic _____ .
5. London is on the _____ Thames.
6. I have a _____ . Give me an aspirin.
7. Don't stand outside in the _____ . Come in.
13. On the shoreline by the sea.
14. Same as trash.
15. I need a _____ to do this job.
17. _____ up this mess!
18. The president must explain his new _____ .
19. Not east.
23. Not west.

ACROSS

3. We have nice white _____ in winter.
8. You must have a _____ balm.
9. Spring is a wonderful _____ .
10. The _____ rays from the sun are harmful.
11. After April.
12. Same as garbage.
16. The way in.
18. The boat is at the _____ .
20. Let's swim in one of the _____ .
21. The money you pay to get in.
22. Same as coast.
24. You have two _____ to see with.
25. After winter.

GRAMMAR SUMMARY

VERBS

SIMPLE PRESENT

to be (Units 1, 2)
Yes, I **am.**
Are you thirty years old?
He/she **is** fine.
Is it on time?
Yes, we **are**
Yes, they **are.**

regular verbs (Units 6, 7, 8)
I/you/we/they **like** baseball.
She/he **works** as a teller.

ending -y, -ies (Unit 9)
What does she **dry?**
She **dries** her hair.

3rd plural -s, -es (Unit 9)
He **irons** his shiart.
She **brushes** her hair.

irregular verbs (Unit 8)
I/you/we/they **have** a cold.
He/she **has** a stiff neck.

want to + verb (Units 6, 7)
I **want to try on** that hat.
She **wants to become** a doctor.

like + noun (Unit 6)
I **like** baseball.

like to + verb (Unit 6)
I **like to dance.**

have to/has to + verb (Unit 10)
I/you/we/they **have to** leave now.
She/he **has to** vacuum.

SIMPLE PAST

to be (Units 5, 6)
I **was** out in the hall.
Where **were** you?
He/she/it **was** at the bike shop.

TENSE CONTRASTS

is/was/will be (Unit 4)
What's the weather like?
What **was** the weather like yesterday?
What **will** the weather be like tomorrow?

there is/are; there was/were (Units 4, 5)
There is one chair left.
There are two tables left.
There was some cough medicine left.
There were some pens left.

PRESENT PROGRESSIVE

is/are +*ing* (Unit 3)
I **am walking** my dog.
Where **are** you **going?**
She/he is brushing her/his teeth.
It **is licking** its paw.
We **are wearing** our boots.
They **are washing** their faces.

PAST PROGRESSIVE

was/were + *ing* (Unit 5)
I **was working.**
What were you **doing?**
She/he **was working.**
They **were watching** TV.

FUTURE

going to + verb (Units 4, 10)
I'm going to help him.

will/won't + verb (Units 4, 6)
I'll take them.
You'll **need** your gloves.
You **won't need** your umbrella.

IMPERATIVES (Unit 8)

Take the elevator.

MODALS

can/can't (Unit 6)
Can you swim?
No, I **can't**./Yes, I **can**.

NOUNS

NOUN PLURALS

-s, -es (Unit 4)
books
glasses

MASS AND COUNT NOUNS

with *some* (Units 5, 7)
I need **some shampoo**.
There **is some shampoo** in aisle 3.
I need **a pen**.
There **are some pens** in aisle 4.

PRONOUNS

SUBJECT PRONOUNS (Units 1, 2, 3)

I'm hungry.
Are **you** ready to order?
He/she is in the yard.
It is licking its paw.
We are wearing boots.
They are combing their hair.

OBJECT PRONOUNS (Units 4, 8)

Can you tell **me** where the office is?
We'll exchange it for **you**.
I don't see **her/him/It/them**.

ADJECTIVES

COLORS (Unit 2)

See that **blue** sign?

NATIONALITIES (Unit 3)

Oh, she's **American.**

POSSESSIVES (Units 2, 3)

This is **my** brother.
Is **your** son eleven years old?
Her husband is 93.
His hair is white.
It is licking **its** paw.
We are wearing **our** boots.
They are washing **their** faces.

DEMONSTRATIVES (Units 4, 6)

I'd like to exchange **this** sweater.
I want to return **these** gloves.
I want to try on **that** hat.
Those shoes are on special.

COMPARATIVES/SUPERLATIVES

with *-er, more* + *than* (Unit 10)
with *-est, most, least* (Unit 10)

I need a **big** box.
Isn't there a **bigger** one?
No, this is the **biggest** one I have.

Is that book **funny/interesting**?
Yes, it's much **funnier than/more interesting than** your book.
This is the **funniest/most interesting** book I have.
What is the **least hated** chore?

IRREGULAR COMPARATIVES AND SUPERLATIVES (Unit 10)

Is Anna a **good** cook?
Is she **better than** Mary?
She's the **best** cook around.

Is Mike a **bad** student?
Is he **worse** than me?
He's the **worst** student I know.

ADVERBS

FREQUENCY (Unit 8)

Do you **always** go straight home?
Sometimes I stop at the store.
How **often** does she have a class?

125

ARTICLES

DEFINITE ARTICLE

the (Unit 1)
Where's **the** post office, please?

INDEFINITE ARTICLES

a and *an* (Unit 3)
She's **a** teacher.
He's **an** artist.

PREPOSITIONS

LOCATION AND DIRECTION
   (Units 1, 2, 5, 7)

It's **on** Green Street.
It's **at** the bookstore.
It's **next** to the bakery.
When is the next flight **to** Atlanta?
When is the next flight **from** Houston?
The salt is **beside** the napkins.
Go **down** the stairs.
Go **up** one flight.

QUESTIONS

QUESTION WORDS AND
   INFORMATION QUESTIONS
   (Units 1, 2, 4, 6, 7, 9)

Where's the hospital?
Who's this?
What's the number?
When is the next plane to Atlanta?
How old is she?
How many tables are left?
How much is this jacket?
How long does it take?
Why?
What's he doing?

QUESTIONS AND STATEMENTS

with *do* (Units 6, 7)
Do you **like to** dance?
What **does** he **do**?
I **don't have** my receipt.
I do, but my son **doesn't**.
Don't you **have** one?

SHORT ANSWERS

with *to be* (Unit 2)
Yes, **I am.** No, **I'm not.**
Yes, **he/she/it is.** No, **he/she/it isn't.**
Yes, **we/they are.** No, **we're/they're not.**

with *do* (Units 6, 7)
Yes, **I/we do.**
No, **I/we don't.**
No, it **doesn't.**

with *can/can't* (Unit 6)
Yes, **I can.** No, **I can't.**

CONTRACTIONS

where's, it's (Unit 1)
Where's Green Street?
It's on the right.

I'm, you're, he's, she's, it's, we're, they're
   (Unit 2)
No, **I'm** not.
No, **he's/she's/it's** not.
No, **we're/they're** not.

CONJUNCTIONS
(Units 3, 6, 7, 8)

I have coupons for the cereal **and** the
   detergent.
I like baseball, **but** I don't like basketball.
He takes biology **because** he wants to
   become a doctor.
Take the elevator **or** the stairs.

INDEX